God's Top Ten:

Taking a Deeper Look at the Spirit of the Ten Commandments

Rev. Frank Julian RN BSN

Infinity Publishing.com
Haverford, Pennsylvania

Copyright © 2005 by Frank Julian

ISBN 0-7414-2860-1

Bible scripture quotations used in this book are from the King James Version and the New King James Version

Published by:

PUBLISHING.COM

1094 New DeHaven Street, Suite 100
West Conshohocken, PA 19428-2713
Info@buybooksontheweb.com
www.buybooksontheweb.com
Toll-free (877) BUY BOOK
Local Phone (610) 941-9999
Fax (610) 941-9959

Printed in the United States of America

Printed on Recycled Paper

Published November 2005

Contents

Dedication

To those who are helping me help the sufferers of HIV/AIDS in Africa, especially through the FAWN organization. You're an answer to my prayers.

Come, get out of the boat. Walk with me on this unchartered course.

Acknowledgments

To my special wife, Peggy, who is the great woman behind the man.

To my best friend, Pastor Pat Bossio, for encouraging me to make my dreams come true and to all my family and faith family. Thanks.

To Grace Lacca for all the typing help.

To Christi Stewart and Therese Faletti for help with the proofreading.

A special thanks to Tiger Whitehead for encouraging me to take the steps needed to write this book and helping me take them.

Introduction

You are about to embark on a fascinating and inspiring journey into the heart of God which will change your mind and transform your heart. This journey will change your views about God, His Holiness, and His Ten Commandments, while transforming your life and your church. This journey is about *a lifestyle of worship* – a lifestyle of being in love with Jesus, one that says, "I want to please the Lord. If something offends Him, it offends me."

This wonderful lifestyle of God's love begins by understanding the spirit – not just the law – of God's Ten Commandments. God gave the law of the Ten Commandments to Moses so that he and the people of God could know God's holiness, His love, and the lifestyle that He wanted His people to live by. Recorded in the Bible in the Book of Exodus, Chapter 20:1-17, they are:

1. I am the Lord your God. You shall have no other gods before me. (Ex 20:2-3)
2. You shall not make for yourselves graven images. You shall not bow down to them or serve them. (Ex 20:4-6)
3. You shall not take the name of the Lord your God in vain. (Ex 20:7)
4. Remember the Sabbath Day, to keep it holy. (Ex 20:8-11)
5. Honor your mother and father. (Ex 20:12)
6. You shall not murder. (Ex 20:13)
7. You shall not commit adultery. (Ex 20:14)
8. You shall not steal. (Ex 20:15)
9. You shall not lie or bear false witness. (Ex 20:16)
10. You shall not covet. (Ex 20:17)

1

To understand God's love and the spirit of His word and commandments, it is important to understand the Ten Commandments not only as individual commands, but also in total context to one another. It is important to tie all the commands together to see the whole picture...this is a lesson I learned well from my nursing background.

A key element to being a nurse is to understand the nursing process. Each semester we focused on one of the stages within the overall process. The first stage was the gathering of assessment data, then planning, implementing, and evaluating the data. It's all part of the process. You do this when looking at a patient. You come up with a prognosis or a plan, and then you actively revise it. Each term we studied an area and a stage of the process. We would have psychiatric nursing classes while we were in our Obstetrics section, which was really kind of revolutionary at that time. But what they wanted you to understand was that the pregnant mother had psychiatric needs, basic mental health kinds of things, and that you should be assessing her psychological status as well as her ability to deliver the baby. But, guess what? I didn't appreciate that kind of program until I got into that sixth term. Then I was able to put it all together. I remember being lost in that first term; it was like saying, "What are they doing? They are talking about babies, while talking about going out to do public health." And I just wasn't getting it.

Sometimes it can be like that in the things of God. We can be mired in the middle of it and not understand it. When we are looking at the Ten Commandments, I think it's neat now to take it apart and then put it all together. It is separated out into parts, into ten parts.

When I was growing up and they were teaching us how to read a book, they'd say, "Read the table of contents, read the preface, read the introduction. Don't just run and start reading Chapter One. Read that jacket; begin to understand a little bit what you are doing." And I used to think that was crazy. I just wanted to dive in, "Let's go with Chapter One, forget about the rest of it." But now when I'm reading a book, I'll go back and look at the table of contents, and see some of the chapters that will be coming. It's really fascinating to learn who the author is, who wrote that book, and to learn about him or her and their background. Nowadays, we have movies, and then movies about the making of the movies. You know, people really get into the process.

Well, just as it is important to apply this process to nursing, to reading a book, and to movies, it is also important to apply this process to the understanding of the Ten Commandments. In this book, we will first take you through each commandment, looking at both the Law *and* the Spirit of each Commandment, and then in the Conclusion I will recap each of the Ten Commandments.

As you will discover while reading this book, there is something truly special behind each of the commandments' teachings which you can apply to your life in this modern-day world. You'll realize, as I did in teaching this message in churches and writing this book, that the life application principles within God's Ten Commandments are found much deeper than a superficial look at the "law" of each commandment. There is more to this than simply, "Thou shalt not steal." You'll begin to ask yourself, and then discover the answer to, "What is God really saying here? What is the deeper meaning in the spirit realm, and how does this apply to me? And why would the author of these Ten Commandments implement each command?" This book will help you answer these questions.

You know, we need to go deeper in study as the people of God, as we mature into that solid believer that God desires us to be. For example, what they would tell us in our nursing program was how special we were, and how fortunate we were that we had four years to study this material instead of just graduating in two years, as in a community college. By taking the extra two years, we were told that we would understand theory well enough so that when we would later be in actual medical situations, such as recognizing that someone had a fever, we would also understand the

3

pathophysiology, the anatomy, and all other dynamics in the human body and mind which would help us to actually treat that person and apply our medical training to their unique condition.

Nevertheless, despite being told of the benefits of being in a four-year program instead of two, we still used to think, "I wish it was just a two-year program." But the reality is that so much of what they said is true. Applying medical knowledge in a way that helps us treat each person uniquely and individually, based not only on their symptoms, but also on who they are as a person, was only made possible by taking that extra two years of training to help us understand medicine and nursing at a much deeper level than the simple "medical facts" that we learned the first two years. If we had only a two-year program, we would have likely learned technical skills, like a robot, which would allow us to look at medical symptoms and say, "Symptoms are 'A;' therefore, the treatment must be 'B' because that's what the medical books tell us." On the contrary, by understanding the principles and theory behind humans and their mental condition (not only their "medical" condition), we are able to truly apply our training in practical situations that addressed their personal needs.

Likewise, if we simply read the Ten Commandments and try to apply them to our lives legalistically, then we will be like legalistic robots who can only repeat and attempt to follow ten rules of God: "Thou shalt not steal, thou shalt not commit adultery, etc.," without ever having a thorough understanding of the spirit of these commandments. With an understanding only of the "law" of the Ten Commandments, but not the "spirit" of the Ten Commandments, we will not only fail miserably in trying to keep those laws, but we will miss the depth and breadth of God's love behind each commandment, and we will never understand God's timeless principles for living that the commandments reveal to us.

But when you understand the spirit of these commandments, they become so much richer, more spiritual, and more meaningful to you. Understanding the principles

4

behind each Commandment will allow you to apply these principles to hundreds and thousands of situations in your life, not just the ten scenarios directly addressed by each law of the Ten Commandments.

As you will discover by reading this book, understanding the Ten Commandments – both the law and the spirit of them – is really about holiness. I really believe it is about the presence of the Lord. I really believe this is why God has called me to write this book. And I know there will be some who say that we should not discuss or try to live by the legal Ten Commandments, because we are no longer under the Law of Moses, and we are not saved by the "law." I know that we are not saved by the law, that we are saved only by the blood of Jesus. I love emphasizing that, and if there is anything that has happened to me while studying, teaching, and writing about God's commandments, it's that I've grown in my appreciation for the blood of Jesus. I realize more than ever that only by the blood of Jesus and His righteousness can we possibly be saved. Because what I've realized in the Ten Commandments is that we really can't keep them. We can't keep a single one of them when we look at the spirit of each of the commands.

There is some point in our life that we make a mistake and we break one of the Ten Commandments. Now, let's be real; Adam couldn't even keep one commandment, let alone ten. Adam broke the law, "Don't eat the fruit," but he ate the fruit anyway. If there was only one law for us to follow, we couldn't keep it. So don't worry that there are ten. You can't even keep one of the ten if you are honest with yourself.

So why does God give us ten? Why didn't he just tell us don't eat any of the fruit? He could have just left one commandment, and Jesus could have died for that, because men were born into sin. They were always going to break the law. The reason that He gave the fuller understanding of the law is because He is a holy God, and it's about relationship. You see, the Bible says that the law IS holy and good. The law is good, and the law is holy – there is nothing wrong with the law. The problem is with us. We needed the savior. We needed Him to die for us.

The beautiful part of the law and the process of understanding it is that it is a guide to who God is, and the things that He likes and approves, versus the things that God disapproves of. Now, this is wonderful to understand this and to have this insight. So when it says, "Thou shalt not steal," and you've got your hand in the cookie jar – hey, God doesn't like this. Don't take money that belongs to my little brother from his cookie jar.

So what a wonderful thing to have an insight into the things that are holy to God. The things that he really took the time out to speak on that mountain. You see, with God, it's all about reconciliation, about peace, and about getting it right. You see, if there is something wrong between you and God, there is a problem. You see, we must deal with it. Although, there are a lot of people that would rather just pull their head under the covers and just ignore it. But I'm the kind of person who'd rather just deal with it. I want to be just free, because I have experienced freedom. I don't want bondage, even for a moment. And if I've failed, if I've missed it, let's get it right. Let's communicate. Let's over-communicate. Let's deal with it because we can get it right. We can work this out.

It's that way with God I believe. He wants us to clean house, to be holy. Now, does the law make you holy? No, the law condemns you; the law shows you where you missed it. Jesus is the one that makes you holy; we praise Him. But do we throw the law away and say, "Well, we don't want to know it. We don't need to know it." No.

I think the law is good, and I have grown in my appreciation even more for the holiness of God. Now, why would God want this book written? To stir up this thing, to say, "I want you to think about the Ten Commandments." The Lord wants us, as a people of God, to know that the Ten Commandments and God's laws are really about relationship. You see, you can't come into his presence with dirty hands and a dirty heart. So does it do good to ignore the

6

law, and not know what it requires? No, it doesn't. Does it do you good to try to keep the law only, and only become legalistic and obsessed about it? I don't think that's it either. Wouldn't the devil want to make you go to one extreme or another, either to become completely lawless, or to be totally legalistic? That's really not it.

What it is, is to be a mature Christian, and to know that if you commit adultery, that is a wrong thing to do. God is not going to blink at that, because there is a consequence to it. The wages of sin is death, and there is something that dies inside of you when you break the law. The wages of sin is death. Is there a remedy? Most certainly: the resurrection of Jesus Christ from the dead. He rose and has ascended on high. He sits on the right hand of the Father, and he ever lives to make intercession for us, so that if we do sin, He is touched with the feelings of our infirmities. He's our high priest. He knows how to intercede for us. He takes the blood to the father, saying "I'm the lamb of God, I've taken away the sins of the world. Here we have got someone crying out for mercy. They know they've broken your law. Forgive them." Like a good lawyer, he gets you off every time. He's our advocate.

The problem is when believers refuse to take advantage of their legal standing in Christ. They don't understand that the term "Plead the blood" is a legal term. When a lawyer "pleads a case," it's a legal term. The blood is legal. God is a God of justice. There is a high court. Things on earth are patterned after God's heavenly home. Moses patterned it after heaven. Don't let anyone tell you that just because they take the Ten Commandments out of a building, that's going to change things. The whole court system is really established on the Judeo-Christian law. This is really what it is based on. You are on the winning side. You are on the winning team. You got it right, regardless of what the media says.

And now, God is bringing you to a new place of maturity, so that you cannot say, "I didn't know that was wrong." Ignorance doesn't work with God. He wants us to know the truth, because the truth will make us free. So when we look at the Ten Commandments, we understand His truths. Over the next several chapters, we will discover those truths – both the law and the spirit of God's Ten Commandments. I hope you will join me now and enter into this deeper walk with me as you discover God's heart, His love for us, His mercy, and the principles of victorious living that are found in God's Top Ten List – the Ten Commandments.

1

Commandment #1:
Are There Other Gods in Your Life?

I am the LORD thy God, which have brought thee out of the land of Egypt, out of the house of bondage. **Thou shalt have no other gods before me.** *Exodus 20:2-3*

In the Book of Exodus, Chapter 19, we read about when God called Moses onto the mountain to speak to Him, to give him the Ten Commandments, and to tell him the rest of the Law for the Jewish people. Before calling Moses to the mountain, God caused Mount Sinai to quake violently, loudly, and in a storm of billowing smoke:

> And mount Sinai was completely in smoke, because the LORD descended upon it in fire: and the smoke thereof ascended as the smoke of a furnace, and the whole mount quaked greatly. And when the voice of the trumpet sounded long, and waxed louder and louder, Moses spake, and God answered him by a voice. And the LORD came down upon mount Sinai, on the top of the mount: and the LORD called Moses up to the top of the mount; and Moses went up. (Exodus 19:18-20)

There is something special to be able to stand in the presence of God. The whole mountain was quaking greatly. The Israelites weren't used to all this: the great noise, the trumpet sounding, thunder, lightning, the smoke, and the mountain quaking. This was something they never experienced before. The trumpet got louder, and God answered Moses by voice. And the Lord came down.

In the midst of all of this, beginning with the very next verse (Exodus 20:1), God began to speak the Ten Commandments to Moses. I want you to understand the drama in which all these words of the Ten Commandments were chosen. The people were in fear and awe of God's power.

It is important to understand that the Ten Commandments didn't make the Israelites a people; they were already a people. They were huddled together in fear of God as all these events occurred before them. They were united together and had a commonality. Then, God spoke the words of the Ten Commandments to His people, beginning with Commandment #1:

> I am the LORD thy God, which have brought thee out of the land of Egypt, out of the house of bondage. Thou shalt have no other gods before me. (Exodus 20:2-3)

This introduction is like the preamble to the constitution. First, constitutions identify the sovereign – who is the king, who is the ruler. Like our constitution, "We the People" – we are a democracy.

In this passage, the King is revealed to the people at a point when they are experiencing unity and commonality as the people and nation of God. He begins to define Himself, "I am the Lord your God who brought you out of the land of Egypt, out of the house of bondage." There is a history here that binds them. The identification of the King, then the history of the people, and then the law of the land will follow. In essence, it is the Israelite constitution.

Once the truth of God's Lordship has been established in the Preamble, God commands allegiance to Himself and none other: "you shall have no other gods before me." This is the first of the Ten Commandments.

In order to understand the people of God, we must understand who God is and to be secure in that fact and that the commandments were given to a people, not individuals.

10

As I began to look at this, I began to understand my own life in God. I see this principle of God, and it excites me to see how God is using my gifts and my talents in the body. My gift, my talent, my calling needs to be expressed in the body of Christ, the church.

In the verse, "You shall have no other gods before me," the word "before" means "in my face." You shall have no other gods in my face, because I am a jealous God. It also suggests "against my face in hostility." If we were to look at the history of Israel, it is in breaking this one commandment that Israel most broke the heart of God. God has feelings. And when they would turn away from Him and go after other gods, it would break His heart and force him to remove His hand from them. He wanted to bless His people; the Bible says He loves them and rejoices over them with singing. But when they were disobedient, He could not bless them.

Imagine how sad it would be for God to watch His children do things that were against the law that He had given them. His children turned away from Him. They persecuted his prophets, like Jeremiah, who tried to talk to them and tell them, "Get right with God, don't have any other gods before you, turn away from those false gods and have the one true God." But they wouldn't listen.

Later in the history of the Jewish people, God expands upon the idea that the Israelites are His people:

> Then the Lord appeared to Solomon by night and said to him, I have heard your prayer, and I have chosen this place for myself as a house for sacrifice. When I shut up heaven and there is no rain, or command the locusts to devour the land, or send pestilence upon my people. But if my people who are called by my name will humble themselves, and pray, and seek my face, and turn from my wicked ways, then I will hear from heaven, will forgive their sins, and will heal their land." (1 Chronicles 7:12-14 NKJV)

When this commandment is broken, there is a process in receiving the healing of God. It is a simple word. It's called "repentance," which is to turn around and follow God instead of following your own wicked ways. The Bible says, "And my eyes will be open, and my ears attentive to prayer made in this place (II Chronicles 7:15)." God's ears are open to your prayers also, but if you hide sin in your heart, the Bible says God will not hear you. You must repent; you must be right with God. You are the people of God. Let us look at this and see and understand. God wants to answer our prayers. He is pleading with them, "If you will follow this pattern, I will hear from heaven and I will heal your land and I will answer your prayers." God wants to bless us! We are his children. He says:

> Now I have chosen and sanctified this house, that my name may be there forever, and my eyes and my heart will be there perpetually. And as for you, if you walk before me as your Father David walked.... You shall not fail to have a man as a ruler in Israel...But if you turn away...and go and serve other gods and worship them... (II Chronicles 7:17-22)

In other words, if you break the first of the Ten Commandments, if you put other gods before me...If you will go and worship things, and idols, etc., then I will uproot them from the land which I have given them, and this house which I have sanctified for my name, I will cast out of my sight and will make it a proverb and a byword of all the people. As for this house, which is exalted, everyone who passes by it will be astonished and will ask, "Why has the Lord done this, to this land and this house." After they would not listen to Jeremiah, God's warnings became true. The enemies invaded, burnt the Temple down, and people passed by with eyes of pity and disgust while wild animals roamed freely through it.

I wanted to show you out of the Old Testament how they were made a people; but if they turned to other gods, God would turn away from them. The Christian has Jesus who died for him. He has His precious blood. Mercy has been shown to him. He receives Jesus Christ into his heart. Jesus becomes the Passover lamb for him. Jesus' blood covers him and the angel of death passes over us, just as the angel of death passed over the Jews, and their firstborn couldn't die. Well, the blood of Jesus is over his doorposts, and the angel of death can't drag him to hell. He is born again. He has life because of the Lamb of God who takes away the sins of the world and he becomes part of the family of God.

Let's continue on as we understand this in light of the Old and New Testament. In the New Testament, Paul carries the same thought, saying, I say then has God cast away his people. (Romans 11:1-5). He says, now I want you to listen to this, because we are the people of God. This is the most precious blessing to be part of the family of God. We've got to count it as precious. We've got to make it our priority. We've got to have no other gods before us; and if we do have other gods, we've got to repent. If you let some other love in your heart, which is very easy to do, repent. We know sin because we know the Law. Sometimes we slip and our affections go after something else. Paul says, "Why do I do the things I don't want to do, and don't do the things I want to do (Romans 7:15)."

But thanks be to God through my Lord Jesus Christ: we have a Savior who delivers us from the times when we slip away from God, so that we can always stay in full relationship with Him and His people. When we are the people of God, our focus has to be on unity, on the body of Christ, on the advancement of the people of God, and on how we can grow together. Look at what God says to Elijah, after he pleaded. "Lord, they did this, they did that, I'm the lone prophet, they seek after my life..." But what does the divine response say to Him and to us: "I have reserved to myself 7,000 who have not bowed the knee to Baal. Even so then, at this present time, there is a remnant according to the election of grace." What he wants to do, he wants to put us in a position in the body of Christ where we know who we are

13

and we're not thumbing down anyone else. It doesn't do any good to find your place in the body, only to put someone else down. You've got to find your place, but if you see another part of the body that isn't in operation, you're not there to say, "Hey, I'm better than them." You're there to intercede for them on their behalf that they may be built up, that they grow and come to the place that God has called them to be.

Now look at Romans 11:13-15. Look at how Paul explains this further. I want you to understand the day we live in. We are living in that time and it's just about ready to happen. We have to be alert as the Christian church, to know our place in the body, and to understand the greater picture, and that includes the Jews of today. They're still the people of God, the remnants of God, those who are of the promise, those who have the seed of faith in their heart...I believe that remnant is alive today, as Paul reminded the Roman Church:

> For if the first-fruits is holy, the lump is also holy. For if the root is holy, so are the branches. If some of the branches were broken off, and you being a wild olive tree were grafted in among them, and with them became a partaker of the root, and fatness of the olive tree, do not boast against the branches. For if you do boast, remember that you do not support the root, but the root supports you. You will then say, 'Branches were broken off that I might be grafted in.' Well said, because of unbelief they were broken off, but you stand by faith. But do not be haughty, but fear. (Romans 11:16-20)

As Christians, we should have a place still of reverence and awe for God. Even as they stood at that mountain when it quaked and shook, they were trembling. We should also tremble at the presence of God, and we should not count our position and place of grace as a people of God as a light thing. This is a marvelous thing, this plan of salvation. It is amazing grace. Don't ever lose your awe of God, but be in fear of Him. Recognize that you are in a special position, and this is not something you should take for granted. He says,

"For if God did not spare the natural branches, he may not spare you either." We should be very cautious and we should walk in the fear of God, and not take everything for granted. Paul says again to the Roman Christians:

> Therefore, consider the goodness and the severity of God. (Romans 11:22a).

Consider the severity, not just the goodness of God. There is a judgment side of God. And if you do not acknowledge that, then you cannot really walk as the people of God. Paul continues:

> On those who fall, severity, but to you goodness, if you continue in His goodness, otherwise, you also will be cut off. And if they do not continue in unbelief, they will be grafted in, for God is able to graft them again. (Romans 11:22b-23).

There is hope for Israel, and they are able to be grafted in again. The time is short, and we will see Jews coming to Christ. If you were cut off out of the olive tree which is wild by nature and were grafted contrary to nature into the cultivated olive tree, how much more will these who are natural branches be grafted into their own olive tree. Paul explains God's inclusive plan and His mercy:

> I do not desire brethren that you should be ignorant...so also Israel will be saved...for this is my covenant with them, that I will take away their sins....they are beloved for the sake of the fathers....for as you were once disobedient to God, you have obtained mercy....they may also obtain mercy, for God has committed....Oh the depth of the riches.. how unsearchable are his judgments...for who has known the mind of the Lord...for of him, and to him are all things. To him be glory forever. (Romans 11:25-36)

I want to conclude with Colossians 1:18: "And He (Jesus) is the head of the body, the church, who is the beginning, the firstborn from the dead, that in all things He may have the preeminence." God must be given the preeminence.

I say to the church, in light of this first commandment: Make him number one in your life, make him God, make him the boss, make him the Lord. Don't have anything else before him. You are breaking the first of the Ten Commandments, and that is a sin. Remove those obstacles that keep you away from God. If there is a sin in your life, get it out of your life. Don't take for granted your position in Christ. Don't think that just because you "got saved" that you can live anyway you want. No, I say holiness is the way to God. I say repent of your sins. I say accept the power of the blood of Jesus to cleanse you of all righteousness, and then understand that you are part of a privileged people as the people of God.

Remember that God has a greater vision of this, and that there are other Christians around the world, and that there is the Jewish remnant that will come in when the fullness of the Gentiles comes in, and together we will all be the people of God. That's what it means to understand the first of the commandments, that He is the Lord our God, and we are the people of God, and we have no other King. He is the sovereign Lord over us. The reason we are called to love everyone, even those we regard as enemies, is because God is forming His people. He reads the heart and He knows those who truly are His, the children of God, which in fact could be an enemy of your's now, but a brother in Christ in the future. You put it all in the hands of God when you love everyone.

2

Commandment #2:
The Attraction of Modern Day Idols and Why They Fall Short

Thou shalt not make unto thee any graven image, or any likeness of any thing that is in heaven above, or that is in the earth beneath, or that is in the water under the earth...Exodus 20:4-6

As I meditated on this commandment, I thought to myself, "this ties in with prayer, Lord." Where is the tie-in with prayer? The Lord showed me that to have an idol is to have something you're praying to other than God. So this talk about prayer is in regards to "idol worship." I believe that the Spirit of God is going to show you something from this commandment that will bless your prayer life. But you have to be open to the Holy Spirit so that you have ears to hear.

Beware of what you are putting before God. The Bible says in Proverbs 3:5, "trust in the Lord with all of your heart and lean not to your own understanding." That is what prayer really is, isn't it? It is a prayer of faith. In James 5:15, it says to pray the prayer of faith, anointing with oil in the name of the Lord and the one who is sick shall be healed. This is a prayer of faith. Your trust must be in the Lord, not in the oil or in the religious ceremony.

It was an awesome moment when the Ten Commandments were given. The people of God really heard the voice of God. They heard the Word; it's called the Decalogue or the ten words. It's not even called the Ten

Commandments in Hebrew. They heard God speak and they saw the mountain tremble and they were afraid:

> Then it came to pass that on the third day in the morning that there were thunderings and lightening and a thick cloud on the mountain and the sound of the trumpet was very loud so that all the people who were in the camp began to tremble. (Exodus 19:16)

This was an unfamiliar thing to them. When you are familiar with something, it doesn't faze you. But when something new is going on, it fazes you. You are alerted to this. They were alerted by these loud noises. They didn't have jets going overhead making all kinds of noises. They heard thunderings and lightening and this trumpet blaring.

> Then Moses brought the people out of camp to meet with God and they stood at the foot of the mountain. (Exodus 19:17)

They were trembling in the presence of God. It is a scary thing. They realized how small they really were and that they're not such a big to-do when you compare yourself with Almighty God. It says in verse 18 that all of a sudden now Mount Sinai was completely in smoke. "What kind of nerve does this God have to tell me not to worship my idols anymore? Is He bigger than my idols? What kind of God is He to tell me not to trust my understanding?"

Is He bigger than you? Can you trust Him? Or do you trust your idols? Maybe your idol is education; maybe your idol is money. What are you trusting in? When He says you can't have any idols it is talking about a deep, deep personal relationship with God. Now John reiterates this in his epistle. 1 John 5:21 says, "Stay away from idols." He is writing to Christians, so it behooves us to examine ourselves. Some would say we are not under the Ten Commandments. Well, go ahead and commit adultery, lie, murder, and steal because you are not under the Ten Commandments. You don't have to keep the law they tell me. Then go ahead and blaspheme the Name of the Lord and covet everybody else's stuff. I think you must keep those commandments. I think it would behoove you to keep those commandments.

The key is that they don't save you. You are saved by faith through grace. Jesus comes into your heart and is the fulfillment of the law in you. He said, I didn't come to abolish it, I came to fulfill it so that you can live it out. You can't live it because of the weakness of your flesh. You can't live it out. God gave Adam one law and he couldn't keep it. ONE! We can't keep the law in our flesh.

So, now let me talk about not having idols. It would behoove you not to have any idols because God is bigger than you. He is Almighty God. He is El Shaddai. He is more than enough. The commandments were a guide to the people of Israel. So, He gave the law as kind of a schoolmaster, to guide them. But because the schoolmaster is gone, the Holy Ghost comes inside of us and we are born again and then the law is written on our hearts.

This doesn't mean we don't have to follow the Word of God anymore. Paul wrote to the Ephesians to quit stealing and work with their hands. That is one of the top ten. Honor your mom and dad. Ephesians chapter 6:1-4 says it will do well for you if you do it. As we enter into this one, you see this is about worship. This is about prayer. The wind and the waves and the storm and the lightening were all about Jesus, as he slept in the boat, yet nothing woke Him up until one of his disciples called out to him, "Master!" (Mark 4:37-38). The call of the disciple woke Him. "Master, help us." The cry of his disciple woke Him, not the lightening, not the wind, not the waves. Peter was a fisherman and he was afraid. But the call of the disciple awoke Him.

Your call will awaken God. But it must be a call in faith. He is God and He is a rewarder of those who diligently seek Him. If you do not have faith in God, your faith is in something else. Either you believe in Him or you don't. And if you don't, you're believing in something else. You're believing in a system, whether it is the economic system, the political system, the media, the intelligentsia, the arts, or some other system of this world.

There are a lot of other things that can be considered idols. Some people say We don't have these carved images that they had in the Old Testament. This is true. We don't have carved images as our idols, yet we nevertheless have more idols today than they ever had: more things to amuse us, more things to entertain us. Let's clean the temple! You are the temple of the Living God!

I just want you to begin to think. I don't want you to be reading this book and thinking that just because you don't bow down to carved wooden images, that you are clearly not an idol worshipper and that God is clearly the only god in your life. I sincerely hope you are in that right place with God as the only god of your life. I have sought to be in that place.

But if you are lusting after things, or people, or experiences in this life, then you are worshipping the idols of lust. In the Bible, James (James 1:13-14) warns Christians about being drawn away by their own lusts. Lusts are just another "idol" that people often fall into the trap of worshipping. Don't fall for the lie. It's all an empty illusion. Idols are an empty illusion. For example, do you idolize being "cool"? Do you have to be cool? You can't serve God wholeheartedly if you can idolize cool. If cool is your idol, then forget about it.

Mount Sinai was completely covered in smoke because the Lord descended upon it in fire. The smoke descended like the smoke of a furnace and the whole mountain quaked greatly. God had to show His power, because He had to show them just how big God was. They were natural people. The Israelites didn't have the Spirit of God. So they had to see with their eyes and feel with their hands and feel it with their legs and say "what's going on here."

I would be afraid if this demonstration of God's power and might happened in the 21st century, let alone 4,000 years ago when they hadn't seen any kind of demonstrations of power. You get in an earthquake and find out if you are really bold and if you are really an awesome person that can handle anything. Can you say "let the roof fall down on me,

I'm not afraid"? I think you'd begin to cry out to God. I believe you would begin to push away any other manmade gods, any other man-made idols, and say "I need God."

Why do we have to be brought to that place? God is our maker and He knows our frame. He knows that we are made of dust and He knows that we are weak. He knows that apart from Him we can do nothing. He reduces us to nothingness in order to allow us to be built back up again in Him. You go through a place of shaking in your life and are brought to your foundation, like a pearl if someone were to pull off every layer until they finally reach that grain of sand. He strips away things that are not of God to get you back to your foundation, so He can start building you back up again. You don't want to be built upon an impure foundation. He doesn't want you trusting in something else while you are trying to go out and serve Him.

Let God show you what He wants. Let Him show you that you cannot lean to your own understanding. Does He still heal today? I believe He does. We had the privilege in South Africa, a partner and I, to see a man healed that was deaf. I stood there. We didn't know what to pray for him at first, because he couldn't tell us because he couldn't hear us. He didn't know what we were asking him. So, I said, "Let's pray for his hearing because I know he's deaf." He was just at the clinic up there and had to have his daughter interpret everything for him. So we laid hands on him and I just kept saying "be opened, ears be opened, in the Name of Jesus, just be opened in the Name of Jesus." Then all of a sudden, the Spirit of God spoke to my heart and I believe it was the Spirit and said "whisper in his ear." So I said let's see if this works and I said "can you hear me?" and he said "yes"!

Wait a minute! I'm a nurse. I have half of the brain that is medical and the other half that's faith and the two were kind of going like the electricity thing buzz, buzz, buzz…I said "You can hear me? I thought you couldn't hear." He said, "Well I couldn't." I thought this guy was pulling one on me. I never saw that happen before, but witnesses confirmed that this man was deaf before and could here now! Praise God for his healing touch and faithfulness!

We are going to see things happen in the future that we have never seen before. We have to get to a place where we are really leaning not to our own understanding and where we don't have any idols or preconceived notions of things, because God wants to move by His Spirit. The man told me that he lost his hearing gradually over time but that he could hear perfectly clear now. Well then, I started to get happy. I'm dragging him. Come on let's go to the clinic; let's tell the doctor!

That sounds like an exciting experience in the Lord. But, I have to tell you something, we were in a sense stripped of everything that we trusted in. We were in a foreign land. We were in a place where there was even a little bit of anti-American spirit. We were in a bad neighborhood where there was a lot of drugs and violence; and we were told not to go anywhere on our own, but to stay with our hosts. God we are here because You sent us and You do what you want to do." When you get to this place, I think that God will be able to move then. I know it's hard here in the United States because you have so much to lean on. In the operation of the kingdom of God, things like that happen. You get to the place where there are no walls to this ministry. You are out there serving God wherever you're at, whatever He wants you to do.

But there is this place of being clothed with God, being clothed with His Glory, inside and out. It is a way of pressing into God. How does this affect your prayer life? When you get to this place, you have developed that deep personal relationship with God.

> And when the blast of the trumpet sounded long and became louder and louder, Moses spoke and God answered him by voice. (Ex 19:19)

You get to this place where you begin to hear the voice of God. Maybe it's through your inner man, inside of you the Spirit of God talking. Maybe it's an angelic Word that is

22

being spoken to you. Maybe it's the audible voice of God. Whatever it is, God's voice will make you change. Something happens inside of you. When His word is spoken to me and it is from God, I remember for years. I can even tell you what was said or what the Lord spoke to me in a prophetic Word.

Now, when someone comes up to you, you think "what did they say?" I don't think that word is from God. What have you hid in your heart? What are you taking time to build into your heart? What preoccupies you? What is the thing that you have hidden in your heart that you might not sin against Him? Is it the Word of God? Is it the voice of God? Are you able in a crisis to go in there and retrieve it?

Let's go to the next part of this command: you shall not make for yourselves a carved image any likeness of anything that is in heaven above or that is in the earth beneath or that is in the water under the sea, you shall not bow down to them and serve them. It becomes a servant kind of a relationship. Exodus 20:5 says, "I the Lord your God am a jealous God."

You have to understand a very important principle: it's called spiritual adultery. The nation of Israel was guilty of adultery, but it wasn't adultery with a woman. It was adultery with other gods. God called that adultery. The prophet Jeremiah spoke of their spiritual adultery because they had worshipped created things in opposition to this command and the fact that He is a jealous God.

It is like a marriage relationship that we have with God, and it's further exemplified in the New Testament in Ephesians 5. It's like a wedding, like a husband and wife. We have a marital relationship with God. When we go after other gods, it's like you are having sex with them in the spirit realm. It is adulterous because there is such an intimate connection with them because you are praying to them. You're giving your heart to them. God will not tolerate that! He will cast you off.

He said, "He will visit the iniquity of the fathers upon their children to the third and fourth generation." Now, look at the next part, "of those who hate me." Don't ever be guilty of hating God. Can you imagine this Word coming from the mountain? This is what they heard. "And the Lord spoke." God spoke these Words while the trumpets were blaring and the mountain was trembling and filled with thunder, lightening, and smoke. The ground was shaking. He said He will visit iniquity to your children, your grandchildren, your great-grandchildren because you hate Me, like a jealous husband.

He takes our relationship very seriously, far more seriously than many in the Christian Church do today, because Christians often don't want to read the Ten Commandments. "If you love Me," Jesus said this in the New Testament, "you'll keep My commandments (John 14:15)." He goes on to say, "He will show mercy to thousands, to those who love Me and keep My commandments." His commandments include the requirement to love, serve, and pray only to God, not to other idols in this world.

3

Commandment #3:
Taking God's Name
(As in Marriage)

Thou shalt not take the name of the LORD thy God in vain; for the LORD will not hold him guiltless that taketh his name in vain.
Exodus 20:7

Commandment #3 has to deal with the name of the Lord. How many know that there is power in the name in the Lord? You cannot take the name of the Lord God in vain, because then you become powerless. "Whoever calls upon the name of the Lord shall be saved (Romans 10:13)."

The church has gotten weak when it comes to faith in the name. Acts 4:12 tells us, "Peter and John speaking up, said 'Nor is there salvation in any other for there is no other name under heaven given among men whereby men must be saved.'"

There's power in the name of Jesus. If you remember anything about this chapter, remember that there is power in the name of Jesus. I want you to remember that you know the name of the Lord and you can have faith in the name of the Lord.

Let's look at the story of the man who was healed, as recorded in Acts 4:7-10. They had respect for the name of the Lord. Even some in the church don't respect the name of the Lord. "In the name of Jesus...." can be in vain if it is not being used in the power in which it is entrusted to you. In Acts 4, Peter looked at the lame man and said, "Look at us: Silver and gold I have none, but what I have I give unto you.

In the Name of Jesus Christ of Nazareth, rise up and walk. And he took him by the right hand and lifted him up and immediately his feet and ankle bones received strength..." This was faith in the name of Jesus! Peter said to those around him, "Men of Israel, why do you marvel at this? The God of Abraham, Isaac and Jacob has glorified Jesus...And his name, through faith in his name, whom you have seen and know, has made him strong. In the presence of you all..."

It is in our presence that we will see signs and wonders if we have faith in the name of Jesus. Religion masks doubt and unbelief. That it what religion is for. All can be guilty of religion. I don't want religion. We fight doubt and unbelief. Those Pharisees were religious. They didn't like what John and Peter did. But because they broke through religion, they got results – it was through faith in the name.

Do you believe in the name of the Lord? I'm talking about really believing. I'm hoping with all of my heart, that within your heart, you are saying Amen. God gave me a scripture one morning when I was preparing to preach this message: Isaiah 64:1-3. Look at what verse 1 says:

> This is my hearts cry, O that you would rend the heavens. That you would tear the heavens open and come back. That you would come down that; the mountain might shake at your presence.

Why do you think the mountain shook when He gave those Ten Commandments? Because He was "present" there. It wasn't because of anything else but that. That mountain couldn't handle the presence of the Lord; it began to shake and quake. That's why some of you, when you get in the presence of God, your hands begin to quake. Some of you even begin to shake. Some of you even fall back – you're under the presence of God. He breaks through; he gets through that hard heart and gives you a touch.

Let's read on. Verse 2 of Isaiah 64 says "As fire burns brush wood, as fire calls water to boil, to make your name known to your adversaries."

You see, the name of the Lord brings the presence of God on the scene. But, it's through faith in the name, not just saying the name of Jesus Christ. Actors use it as a cuss word in the movies. They use it as a piece of dirt to trample on, and they rub it into the ground and make it as if it's a worthless piece of trash. But I want to tell you something: it is the name above every name that can be named. At the name of Jesus, every knee is going to bow and every tongue confess that Jesus Christ is Lord to the glory of God the Father. And, if they don't want to do it, they're going to have to do it, on the other side of glory (see Philippians 2:9-11).

But, you say, "I bow to the name of Jesus." We're talking about growing in Christ here. When the enemy wants to come in your life like a flood, and he wants to destroy your life because you're out serving God, you've got to know that there is power in the name of Jesus. You've got to really believe in the name of Jesus.

I want to tell you something. There were some guys that saw Paul casting out devils in the name of Jesus, and they tried to cast out devils themselves, by saying, "In the name of the Jesus that Paul believes in." The devils came out of those guys and they ripped them to shreds and they ran out of that place naked and bleeding (Acts 19:13-16). You can't do it in faith in the name that Pastor Frank preaches; nor can I do it in the faith that you have. You must come to believe that there is power in the name of Jesus. Mark 16 says that if you lay hands on the sick in the name of Jesus, they will recover. The demons WILL flee. To the Corinthian Christians, Paul wrote:

> But as it is written: "Eye has not seen, nor ear heard, nor have entered into the heart of man the things which God has prepared for those who love Him."
> But God has revealed them to us through His Spirit. For the Spirit searches all things, yes, the deep things of God. (I Corinthians 2:9-10)

What Paul does is puts the statement of faith AFTER the quotation. "But it has been revealed to us by the spirit." In Isaiah 64, Isaiah puts the statement of faith BEFORE he says that. He believes that the mountain quaked because the Lord was showing his presence. The eyes have seen it because God was on the scene. He was present. He wants you to believe that when you speak His name in faith, mountains will get up and go into the sea. A lot of people will say, "No that's just a big faith message and you can't take the Bible literally." Take it literally! Go ahead and believe. Go ahead and believe that if you've got a mountain in your life, that it can get up and it's gotta go into the sea. That little mustard seed of faith that you have is able to break through that granite, that hard substance, that crusty thing, and just make it dissolve and be removed and it says, "to make the mountain be a plain, and to cause the valleys to be filled in." God wants us to believe in the name of Jesus!

If you look at the Ten Commandments in Exodus 19, you're going to see something very special here. It says:

> And it came to pass on the third day in the morning, that there were thunders and lightnings, and a thick cloud upon the mount, and the voice of the trumpet exceeding loud; so that all the people that were in the camp trembled. And Moses brought forth the people out of the camp to meet with God; and they stood at the nether part of the mount. And mount Sinai was altogether a smoke, because the LORD descended upon it in fire: and the smoke thereof ascended as the smoke of a furnace, and the whole mount quaked greatly. And when the voice of the trumpet sounded long, and waxed louder and louder, Moses spake, and God answered him by a voice. (Exodus 19:16-19)

They heard the voice of God. I want you to think about this for a moment. Meditate on this. Don't take this for granted. The mountain was quaking and shaking. Now you can look at that in retrospect and think, "Wow, that's cool." But, I want you to think what it would have been like to be one of those Israelites at the foot of that mountain. You see there were people in Los Angeles when there was an earthquake, and they were trembling in fear at not knowing what was going on. They were in the middle of the night, and some of the people told their story. What a fearful thing it is to be living through an earthquake. It was a fearful thing for the Israelites to be living through this moment in time, and God wanted them to see His majesty. He wanted them to see just a little bit of His power being manifested. He wanted them to see what it would be like for His presence to come down on that mountain. I'm asking you to think what it would be like for His presence to enter into your life. Some things will break away; other things will break away. It's going to happen, to bring you to that place of purity. God wants a pure and holy people so that the power of God can flow through them.

Now, God gave two great commandments. In Matthew 22:37-40, He gave these commandments and I want you to see something in them. They are:

"Thou shalt love the Lord thy God with all thy heart, and with all thy soul, and with all thy mind. This is the first and great commandment. And the second is like unto it, Thou shalt love thy neighbour as thyself. On these two commandments hang all the law and the prophets."

Now if you will study the Ten Commandments, you will see that the first four commandments are about loving and honoring God:

1. The first commandment is that you shall have no other Gods. It shows the oneness of God – He is the only God.
2. The second commandment is that you will have no idols, no false worship.
3. The third commandment: His name will not be taken in vain, because it's Holy. It's the name of God. It sets Him apart.

4. The fourth commandment is to honor God's day, the Sabbath. You're going to spend that day in spiritual renewal, doing nothing but meditating on God, and resting and allowing yourself to be filled in preparation to go back for the other six days. You're being filled with God; you're setting yourself apart.

Now, the last six commandments deal with the second of Jesus' commandments, to love your neighbor as yourself. These commands tell you to not steal from your neighbor, do not covet your neighbors' possessions, do not commit adultery with your neighbor's spouse (or against your own spouse), do not kill your neighbor, do not lie to them, and honor your mother and father. This is all relational. This is between you and other humans. The first four are with God.

So, if you love God with all of your heart, you'll honor him, you'll have no idols, you'll worship him and him alone, and you'll keep his day holy. And, if you love your neighbor as yourself, you're going to follow the other six.

Now, we want to go deeper into this. Because if you go in deeper, you're going to come out stronger. You're going to come out like gold.

Now listen, You shalt not take the name of the Lord thy God in vain. This is what Paul prayed concerning the Thessalonian church:

> Therefore we also pray always for you that our God would count you worthy of this calling, and fulfill all the good pleasure of His goodness and the work of faith with power, that the name of our Lord Jesus Christ may be glorified in you, and you in Him, according to the grace of our God and the Lord Jesus Christ. (2 Thessalonians 1:11-12).

Paul is praying this prayer for the Thessalonians, but I pray this for myself. He says, "Therefore, we also pray always for you, that our God would count you worthy of this calling and fulfill all the good pleasure of His goodness and the work of faith with power." When I pray this for me, something good happens inside of me. I pray that God would count me worthy of his calling, and that He would fulfill His good pleasure and his goodness and His work of faith in power in me.

I just get greedy sometimes for the things of God. I just want more. I'm hungry. I want to have His faith working in me in power. And I'm not there yet, so I have to pray this. I want this. I'm hungry. It's the goal I press on towards the prize. I haven't arrived. I'm seeking after it. Get hungry for more of God, want it with me, let's take it together! Amen.

Now read verse 12: "That the name of our Lord Jesus Christ may be glorified in you." It says "in you," but I turn it around and say "in me." I want the name of the Lord Jesus Christ to be glorified in me, and I in Him. I want this union according to the grace of our God and the Lord Jesus Christ.

Now, what does it mean to want the name of the Lord to be glorified in you? I believe this. I believe that we are to walk worthy of the calling by which we have been called. And the way that you take the name of the Lord in vain is by living a life that is not worthy.

You're going deeper. I want to point it out to you that you can't keep the commandments; you can't keep them. That's why you need grace. You can't live by the law. You say, "But I'm going to try." I say, "Good, good, let's all press on towards the prize." That's why I thank God for Jesus Christ and His precious blood, and it's why I worship Him. The more you get into the Word of God, the more you will understand the grace of God. It says, "grow in the grace and in the knowledge of our Lord and Savior, Jesus Christ."

The deeper you go, the more you praise him! But, when you hunger to not take the name of the Lord in vain and understand your shortcomings, I believe He empowers you and brings you in a little closer and helps you live that life that's a little more worthy.

Yes, we've got to live a life that is worthy. We've got to work worthy of this high calling, that the name of the Lord be glorified. My name is Frank Julian, and I've got the same name as my father. There was something in our family that

31

we wanted to have a good family name. We didn't want the name of our family to be trashed. But that was important to us.

Guess whose name you are called by? You are called by the name of the Lord. You are a Christian. You bear the name of Jesus Christ; and if you don't live a life worthy and walk worthy, you bear that name in vain. You bear that name for nothing. You treat that name as trash. But no, you've got a destiny. Jesus said, "blessed is He who comes in the name of the Lord." I am passionate about this because I see it, as I meditate on it. I want to keep this commandment.

Make your life count for Jesus, knowing what He wants you to do, and then do it in the name of the Lord. He says, "whatever you do in word or in deed, do it in the name of the Lord." And so when you go about doing something, remember whose family you are a part of. Do you want to disgrace the family name? I don't think so. You love the Lord. But let's go a little farther; let's press on a little deeper. Let's understand these Ten Commandments as guidelines, the constitution for our family, if you will. Be so in love with God that you just flow in this, because He's given you grace, He's given you the Holy Spirit to help you walk it out.

I can tell you, that more than ever, we've got to believe that there is power in the name of the Lord Jesus. More than ever you have to walk a life that is worthy of the name. Because if you're under condemnation, and you've been sinning, like Samson, you've just got a haircut. It's going to be awefuly hard when the enemy comes on you, That temptation just rises up against you and if you have been brought to a weak place, you'll succumb to it.

But let's choose together to be strong. Let's choose together to walk a life worthy of the name. Because the Bible says, "they know their God and shall be strong in exploits." That's what I want to do in my life, to do exploits in God. And I believe that's what God wants. If we keep growing and growing, we get to a place and say – what's next God? Eye has not seen, ear has not heard, but by the spirit of God, His plans will be revealed to us.

I want to encourage you to get off that couch and to get back into the Word of God. Allow yourself to be saturated with the Word. Be filled with the Word of God. Be filled with the Spirit of God. Be filled with the Spirit of faith. Be filled with the grace and knowledge of our Lord, so you can take the name of Jesus and yield it like a sword. The enemy must bow to His name. The enemy will come against you one way. But the Bible says when you hold up the name, the enemy will flee from you in seven ways.

Satan will work through people, and he will come against you and try to disturb the peace. We have to know that there is power in the name of Jesus, that there is power in the blood of Jesus, because greater is the spirit that is within us, than he that is within the world. We have to fight spiritual warfare. If you want to do great things in God, do you think Satan is going to sit back and let you do it? He will fight against you.

But, there's something you can do against Satan. Be strong in the Lord. Be strong in the name. Use the name. It's a time for us to pick up our spiritual weapon. When you see the enemy rise up against you, lift up a standard against him and he will have to flee in the name of the Lord. It will cause the mountains to quake if you have faith in the name. This is the time for you to be spiritually alert.

I want you to think about what you are going through. I want you to think about the mountain that's in your life. I want you to think about the obstacle that maybe you let roll over you. This is a time for you to back it up and command it to go in the name of Jesus. Now, I'm going to give the command of faith in the name of Jesus. I want you to see that lame guy at the city gate from Acts 3, how Peter pulled him up, and he was healed in the name of Jesus Christ. Now, I want you to see your situation. I don't care if it looks crippled and dead and that there is no possible chance of it being healed – God can do it through faith in the name, through his presence coming on the scene. Pray and believe for your need. Take this moment to do it before going to the next chapter.

4

Commandment #4:
Only Special People Don't Have to
Work Every Day

Remember the Sabbath day, to keep it holy. Six days shalt thou labour, and do all thy work: But the seventh day is the Sabbath of the LORD thy God: in it thou shalt not do any work, thou, nor thy son, nor thy daughter, thy manservant, nor thy maidservant, nor thy cattle, nor thy stranger that is within thy gates: For in six days the LORD made heaven and earth, the sea, and all that in them is, and rested the seventh day: wherefore the LORD blessed the Sabbath day, and hallowed it. Exodus 20:8-11

Commandment #4 is the entering into the rest of the Lord. That is such a key part of Christianity. So many Christians fail to understand this.

We are talking about the presence of the Lord. To be in the presence of God it defies all words. The Bible tells us in 1 Corinthians 13 that knowledge will pass away. When you're in the presence of God, no one will need to tell you any more about him. There's going to be this communication, this experiential knowledge, and all our questions will be answered. This is the eternal rest promised to believers. The "rest of the Lord" in this life is described in the Book of Acts:

> Repent therefore, and be converted that your sins may be blotted out, so that the time of refreshing may come from the presence of the Lord. (Acts 3:19)

I want you to understand from the idea of the Sabbath and the Sabbath rest. What does it mean to enter into the rest of God? If you are not living by faith, you are violating the Sabbath. So, when you read this and feel that you are not resting in God, don't be condemned; but come away with an understanding of the Sabbath rest. Come away with an understanding of your position in Christ. And when you fail to enter into that rest, go ahead and acknowledge it and get right with God, and repent.

The Bible says, "the Kingdom of God is love, joy, and peace in the Holy Spirit." If we are not in peace, guess who is wrong. Not God, but us. We're missing it somewhere. Are we in worry, in fear, or in lack of knowledge? People perish for these various reasons. Maybe the Lord is drawing you in to understand something? Maybe that's why you are not in peace. We have to dig in the word. At other times, God will just sneak up on you and show you something, which you were neither searching for nor expecting.

One time I visited a person from the church in the hospital. I didn't want to do it, but the Holy Spirit moved me to do it. The person was overjoyed when I entered the room, and the presence of God was so strong. I felt joy. That is the rest of the Lord. The rest is to enter into the presence of God. It is not what the Pharisees made it into: to sit there and do nothing for 24 hours.

Why is the Sabbath so important to the Jewish religion? It is the first of two commandments that are spoken in the "positive." All the others are "thou shalt not do this." Only two are positives: this one, and the command to honor your father and mother.

Remember, the Ten Commandments are divided into two sections: Commandments 1 through 4 deal with loving God with all your mind, heart, soul and strength. Commandments 5 through 10 deal with loving people – loving your neighbor as yourself. Jesus said if you keep these two commands, you fulfill all the law and the prophets.

Let's try to understand. What does this actually mean, the Sabbath? It does not mean to do nothing. It actually means "to rest," to cease from your labors. It means rest. To stop. Now, it's very important that you understand the depth of what God is trying to say here, and we can better understand that from the prophet Ezekiel:

> More over, I also gave them my Sabbath to be a sign between them and me that they might know that I am the Lord who sanctifies them. (Ezekiel 20:12)

He wanted it to be a sign. Now, this is what is going to really attract people to God. You see, the Jews covet a sign. They want to know their God is real. And not just the Jews, but a lot of people in your life. They want to know that your God is real. And, you know what? He established these Sabbaths and had a way of working it out. That if they picked up the manna on Friday and they took an extra day's worth, that it would last; because he planned the Sabbath. That is an amazing sign. So they had enough for Saturday, because they were not to go out on Saturday to collect food.

Most commentaries say that the Sabbath is a sign of you being a king. It was never heard of that you should sit down and take ease the whole day long, that you don't have to talk to a boss, even the man servants and the maid servants. Your boss doesn't have control. Everybody's a king; everybody's their own boss on Saturday. That was an imitation of God; he rested.

That is awesome that nobody was to work on that day. They were the ones that were always to be waited on, even though they were not waiting on one another. They were to rest. They were to rest physically, emotionally, mentally, and they were to worship. They were to be refreshed spiritually.

The Jews distorted the sign. They made it burdensome. They developed hundreds of laws, and Jesus was frustrated. Let's read some of his frustrations from the gospels:

> Have you not read in the law that on the Sabbath the priests in the temple profane the Sabbath, and are blameless. Yet I say to you that in this place, there is one greater than the Temple. If you had known what it meant, "I desire mercy, and not sacrifice," you

would not have been condemned. For the Son of Man is Lord even of the Sabbath. (Matthew 12:5-8)

What man is among you who has one sheep, if he falls in the pit on the Sabbath, will not lay hold of it and lift him out. How much more valuable then, is a man than a sheep. Therefore, it is lawful to do good on the Sabbath. (Matthew 12:11-12)

You see they had to get it into proper understanding, to begin to understand the "sign." Let's look at another of Jesus' teachings about the Sabbath:

The Sabbath was made for man, not man for the Sabbath. This is where we get confused thinking that the law is going to be the thing to save us, rather than the law being there for our own good, as our guideposts to direct us. (Mark 2:27-28)

Again this was very important to Jesus. He spent a lot of time correcting them about the Sabbath. There is a point here that I want you to understand and I believe it the reason for this teaching. He goes on to say in verse 28, "The Son of Man is Lord also of the Sabbath."

In Mark 3:4, He asks of them, "Is it lawful on the Sabbath to do good or to do evil, to save life or to kill?" He wanted to show them how ridiculous they had made it, that he's got to ask a question like that. So also, some of you have asked me the questions, "Do we have to keep the Sabbath? Do we have to do no work on Sunday, because we observe the day of rest on Sunday?"

I want to ask you why aren't you worshipping the Lord on Sunday? What becomes your reason for not coming to church? Is it because your wife is sick in the hospital and you have to be there at her side? Or is it because you stayed up late Saturday night, and really needed to sleep in? I want to ask you something even deeper here.

Because I am a nurse, I had to work a lot of weekends. And sometimes I would think about it, and I did have to miss a lot of church. But there was something compelling me to do good. It felt good to do good? Was I working 7 days a week, 12 hours a day? Was I refusing to obey the idea of what the Sabbath meant? No. That's wrong. You might say, "But I have to support my family." That's like taking two doses of manna, because you are trying to hoard it, instead of trusting in the Lord.

When you live by faith, when you walk by the idea of the Sabbath rest, you have ceased from your labors and entered into his rest. If you are so busy, that you don't have time to come to church to worship God and allow the God-ordained principle to operate in you, to refresh your soul and to renew your mind, then you are violating the Sabbath.

Where is your heart? Are you serving God or mammon? It becomes a heart issue. God does want your heart. He gives us these ideas so that we wake up to see where we are at with God. He wants you, and deep inside you want Him. But you are not trusting Him; and, therefore, he cannot bless you because you have tied his hands.

Now, let's read another passage. Read what Jesus says about the Sabbath:

> Moses therefore gave you circumcision, not that it is from Moses, but from the fathers, and you circumcise on the Sabbath. If a man receives circumcision on the Sabbath so that the Law of Moses should not be broken, you are angry because I have made a man completely well on the Sabbath? (John 7:22-23)

Do not judge according to appearances, but make a righteous judgment. I am asking you to go deeper. I'm asking you to look into your heart and to say, "Do you trust God?" Are you able to trust in God? He wants to be your father, he wants to be your provider. He wanted to be the king over Israel, but they wouldn't let him be. He did not want the monarchy. David was anointed as king, but when they got into the generational thing, about who becomes king – the firstborn son, etc. That was not like the anointing that came upon David. Even under Solomon it became more and more diluted. His idea was for a theocracy, a nation run by God's direction.

And that is how your life is to run. That's why he got angry at them when they refused to keep the Sabbath, because they were all about their own life. They were not about living for God. It was a sign.

Now, I want you to hear what some say about the Sabbath. They say the Sabbath was a day of privilege. Every person could live like a king, free from work and obligation to anyone. It was a jubilee. It was a sign even of heaven. It was a sign of their eternal life, to be in the presence of God, to have ceased from the labor of life itself. That is renewing.

We need to think about heaven a lot more than we do. We get way too entangled in this life and the cares of this life. That chokes off the Word of God and we become fruitless, because we care so much about the things of this life. God wants us to be thinking of Him. He wants to be our first love. You have got to be in love with Jesus to the point where you are filled with the Holy Spirit, and you are walking in the Spirit. Then, you will not fulfill the lusts of the flesh.

You must reevaluate your priorities. But if you are really saying that Sunday is the only day that you sense that, because you've been in church in the morning and evening, then I praise God even for that in your life. On Tuesday you've got to think about what happened on Sunday, remembering the presence of the Lord, so that that presence can come in you. Then a time of refreshing, even on Tuesday, can be felt.

Now, I want to tell you something by looking at Hebrews 4. If you refuse to listen to what I am saying to you here, you are on perilous ground in your relationship with God. Let's look at this important passage of scripture:

> Therefore, since the promise remains of entering His rest, let us fear, lest any of you seem to have come short of it. (Hebrews 4:1)

There should be fear of the Lord in your life. If you are not entering into rest with God, then you are missing it. You are missing one of the Ten Commandments. You need to get right with God. You need to repent. You need to seek forgiveness from God. Because you are living your life, you are not allowing Jesus Christ to be Lord of your life. It's all about you. He said, "If you have not entered into this rest (Hebrews 4:2)," For indeed the gospel was preached to us as well as to them, but the word which they heard did not profit them, not being mixed with faith of those who heard it.

You can hear all the Word of God you want. But if you let it go in one ear and out the other, then it won't help you. You must have a relationship with Jesus Christ. Religion will not save. And I don't care how pretty you make it look. Legal observances will not save. It is a matter of faith. You have got to hear the Word of God, and it has got to be mixed with faith to do you any good. You can weep and wail before God and cry him a river. All you're going to be is wet, if there is no faith in that. People can wail up a storm. That will profit you nothing if it's not mixed with faith.

Do you really believe in God? Has He got the lordship of your life, the reigns of your life? Read this:

> For we who believed as He has said, "So I have sworn in my wrath, they shall never enter into My rest." Although the works were finished from the foundation of the world, for he had spoken in a certain place of the seventh day, in a way and God rested on the seventh day from all his works, " and again in this place, "They shall not enter into my Rest." There is some who will not enter the rest. It goes on to say, "Since therefore it remains that some must enter it, and those to whom it was first preached did not enter it because of disobedience. (Hebrews 4:3-6)

Obedience is better than sacrifice. Because if you obey, then you don't have to offer the sacrifice. The sacrifice is for the sin of disobedience. Obedience is better than offering the

41

sacrifice is what he is saying. Obedience is rest. I'm not happy when I'm not obedient. Things are going on inside of me, because my everything is God and I've got to get right with him. Once I get it right, then I have the rest; the peace that passes understanding that allows me to walk in the Spirit. When I'm not walking in the Sabbath rest, guess what? Everybody knows it, starting with me. Let's finish this with verses 7-10:

> David designated a certain day calling it Today, "Today if you hear his voice, do not harden your heart." For if Joshua had given them rest, they would not afterwards have spoken about another day. Therefore, there remains a rest for the people of God. For he who has entered into His rest, has himself ceased from his works, as God did from his.

Ask yourself these questions. Are you still out to prove who you are? Is it still about you and your works? Or, are you living a surrendered life and really coming into a place of rest, and saying, "God what is it really that you want me to do?" Verse 11 continues:

> Let us therefore be diligent to enter the rest, lest anyone fall according to the same example of disobedience."

This is for you. All of us need to understand this. God forbid, lest any of us fall, through our disobedience. God is calling us to obedience. Obedience is rest, obedience to the Spirit of God, obedience to the Word of God. That's what it means to enter the Sabbath rest, and if you find someone who says, "I don't want to hear the word of the Law; I don't want the word of the Old Testament because it's all the Law." Say to them, "Is there lawlessness in you?" Or, are you not willing to understand what it means to be obedient? That's really what breaking the law is: disobedience.

You see, the Bible says that Jesus rose from the dead and entered into God's glorious presence. Jesus said, "It is finished." He accomplished the Father's will.

Let's serve and be obedient and do what we can do, while we have the chance to do it. You're going to have rest and joy and you'll enter into the place where the glory of God comes upon you. Others will see that you are serving the Lord. You are a witness for God, and YOU become the "sign." You become the sign of the Sabbath rest. You become the sign of what heaven is going to be like.

5

Commandment #5:
Honor the Life-Givers:
Mother and Father

Honour thy father and thy mother: that thy days may be long upon the land which the LORD thy God giveth thee. Exodus 20:12

There is a book by Gary Smally called "Blessing." What it tells us is that we all crave the blessing of our parents. You want the blessing. People will go through life panting for the blessing if they didn't get it. That will be the central theme of their life, to feel that somehow they are pleasing to mom and dad, especially if the blessing has been withheld. And I speak to you as parents, do not withhold the blessing from your children. Do not be manipulative in that way.

Now, it is very biblical for the parents to bless the sons. We see that in Abraham, Isaac, Jacob, Joseph and it goes on. We can see that. There is a blessing that comes from the parents. In our generation, it might not be as formal as calling the children to the death bed and blessing them. But I want to tell you something. My kids know that they want to please me. We have such a relationship that Angela, my daughter, would say, "Oh, it makes me so mad that I want your approval." But, it is a part of her.

They've known me as father, as dad, and there has been love and fun in the home. So I really have to be cautious, because I know that she does want to please me. I know that she wants my blessing. I don't want it to be manipulative. I want to be God-centered on that. I want her to develop independence and grow and mature into a godly woman as I thank God she is. But it is very evident when we honor our mother and father, we are really developing our relationship with God. This is a commandment that has a promise that goes with it: "Honor your mother and your father that your days may be long upon the land that the Lord your God has given you."

First of all, understand the word honor. Let's take this apart a little bit. The word honor comes from the Hebrew word for "fat." I thought that was hilarious. What it really means is "heavy" or "fat." Because the people who were heavy or fat in Bible days were rich. They had the money. They were respected. The affluent ones prided themselves on being heavy and fat. And believe it or not, that's where that root word comes from. "To honor," "to revere," "to respect" comes from the word "heavy" or "fat" based on that Hebrew word.

This is not a promise that you can say, well, I'll keep it if they are "worthy" of my honor. You're told to honor them whether or not they are worthy of that respect. Because it does something in you. When you dishonor them, guess what? You're disobeying the commandment. YOU feel that you are not right with God.

It's important to understand that God is seen as the life-giver and so are the parents. That is the reason for the honor, and why God would stress that so much. Remember that the first four commandments have to do with loving God, and the next six commandments have to do with loving your neighbor as yourself. The first people in the relationship between man are your mother and father, who you must learn to love as mom and dad. You've got to love God, then you've got to learn to love your neighbor as yourself. The first neighbors to love are your mother and father.

Now, why is this so? Because God is seen as the life-giver. And that's why He is respected; He gave you the gift of life. Well, your parents, as His representative, gave you the gift of life. That is one reason why it is believed in Hebrew scriptures that God would want you to honor them, because they are the life-givers to you. They gave you life. You are to honor them for that.

It has been shown in modern studies that if someone does not know how to respect their mother and father, their relationship with God is damaged. If your parents mistreated you and you think that God is rotten, that He will beat you and only see you in a condemning way, then it's going to take more of an effort to learn to love God than for the one who was raised in a godly home where there was love, respect, kindness, and peace shown to them. I think that is obvious. We can take it to the next level and say that it does affect our relationship with our Heavenly Father if our earthly parental relationship is distorted.

When I was growing up, I didn't know we were in a dysfunctional family. I thought relatives fighting with each other was just being "Italian." They'd snub one another and not talk with one another for a year. Then I found out, "Oh, that's dysfunctional." All that passive-aggressive behavior is not very functional, but that's all they knew.

Maybe you are thinking your parents were dysfunctional, that there is no hope for you because it affects your relationship with God. No. That's why Jesus came to the cross. That's why Jesus is here to redeem you, to buy you back, to transform you, to take you from one level of glory to another. If you had an impaired relationship with your parents, and they were not loving, and they did not teach you and instruct you in principles and precepts, and spend time with you, and live life with you...if they didn't do that, I want to tell you something: if you will begin the process, healing will take place! If all you do is blame them, you will never get healed.

I know people that just blame mom and dad by saying my mother didn't love me, my father didn't love me, that's why I'm no good. With God, you can get out of that mind-set and get on the road to healing. There can be a process that develops inside of you, but you've got to be willing sometimes to go into those areas maybe that are painful. Because of Jesus' horrible sacrifice, because of the price that he paid, by his wounds we are healed. We can trust a God who loves us, we can go into that dark cloud with Jesus. He can heal even the worst of atrocities that a parent can commit to their child. God can do it. God can somehow make it right when it was so wrong.

Maybe you feel you could not get your father's blessing, or your mother's blessing. Maybe you feel you were the black sheep of the family. You can get the blessing from God. I believe He can redeem it, and He can be your Heavenly Father. You can feel that you are pleasing to God. You can hear those words that He spoke to Jesus, "This is my beloved Son, in whom I am well pleased." You can hear that kind of love the Father has for you, that divine word, spoken to your heart, that you are His beloved son, in whom he is well pleased.

I would encourage you to begin thinking along these lines. There are promises that are given with this verse. It says if you will honor your mother and father, it will go well with you in the land. There are two meanings to this. Actually, it says here that "your days will be long upon the land which the Lord your God is giving you." That was really important to the Jews. They were not in the promised land yet. Studies have shown that if the family breaks down, it won't be long before the society begins to have all kinds of problems. For the Jews that meant that they wouldn't remain in the promised land.

God knew it before today's modern psychologists, because He says it will go well with you in the land if you respect your mother and father. You're going to have a better society. Isn't that amazing that God knew that? And He even said to them that you will be able to live a long time in that promised land. I know you've heard this before, but I want you to think about it. This is such an important truth for those rearing children or grandchildren. All of society hinges on this. Think of some of these blended families that have kids from three different marriages. I'm not condemning them; it's the reality. Maybe there has been something that has been lost in the strength of that home. But if we have failed, He is our forgiver, our redeemer, and our healer.

Let's go on and examine this even further. God wants to show us just how much He thinks of this commandment. Consider the following scriptures:

> Whoever strikes his father or mother, shall be put to death. He who curses his father or mother, shall be put to death. (Exodus 21:15-17)

> Everyone of you shall revere his mother and father, and keep my Sabbaths; I am the Lord your God. (Leviticus 19:3)

> For every one who curses his father or his mother shall be put to death. He who has cursed his father or mother; his blood shall be upon him. (Leviticus 20:9)

Cursing one's parents was a capital crime. You wouldn't know that in this society, but back then it was that important. I must lay that foundation before we begin to look at it in the New Testament. I want you to understand that it was a benchmark in the Jewish life. That's where we get in our day the stereotypes about the Jewish mother. There's still something special about the Jewish mother.

Another very important point that the commentaries brought out was that back then, societies were very partriarchal, honoring only men. But not in the Jewish society where God commanded honor your father AND your mother. They were to honor the father and mother so much that when Jesus was hanging on the cross, he remembered his mother, to provide for her. That's how embedded it was in the Israeli's life, to honor their father and mother.

With that, I want to go into the New Testament, and I want to begin to show you what Jesus said about it.

> If anyone comes to me and does not hate his father and his mother, his wife and children, brothers and sisters, yes his own life also, he cannot be my disciple. (Luke 14:26)

49

Now, I want you to read this with fresh understanding, maybe in a way that you've never heard it before. You need to sit and spend a moment to understand the depth with which the commandment went forth when it was spoken by God Himself on Mt. Sinai to honor your mother and father. So how can Jesus, the Messiah, tell them to hate their mother and father? Does this Bible contradict itself? No.

Look more closely at the verse. It says "Unless you hate your...whoever does not bear his own cross...cannot be my disciple." There is a laying down of your life, even to the point of hating your own self. Now, Jesus does not want you to be a masochist. He doesn't want you to hurt yourself. You were not meant to torture yourself to die to self. All you have to do is to die to self by choice. Say, "I will do the will of God."

And really when you look at this idea of hating your mother and father, it really means in comparison to your love of the Lord. You are to love the Lord, and you are to love everybody, including your mother and father who are in a special, revered place. But if you come to a place where your homes were split in half, some believing Jesus to be the Messiah, and some not believing He is the Messiah, then He said you've got to choose Me, even over this revered tradition and the Word of God.

I would say to you, in the light of everything said, if your parent does not want you to follow Jesus, then you do have to choose Jesus, even over the great love that you might have for your mother or father, to the point where your mother or father might accuse you of hating them. Now, I didn't come out of a Jewish background, but I came out of a denominational background. They didn't understand my desire to just follow the Holy Spirit and to be led by the Holy Spirit and to walk in the things of God. I really did try to honor them and to love them, but there was always a strain there. I wasn't obeying them. They thought they were right, and I grieved them. It hurt me to hurt them. There is a cross in Christianity.

Jesus said you must take up your cross. I think that sometimes that's the stuff that hurts the most. It hurts more than even physical pain. The soulish pain that you are not pleasing your mother or father. For some of you, maybe it's your children: you are to love Jesus more than your children. Your children say, "You're crazy, what are you doing going on that mission trip? You're 65 years old!" But you really have to do it, if you feel that is what God is calling you to do. Or maybe some of your children might tell you that you are getting too involved in church, praying all the time, getting involved in the Bible. You have to understand this idea and say to your children "I love you, but I love Jesus more."

I bring this out because some people use that as a copout for loving their mother and father. And Jesus addressed this:

> Then came the scribes and Pharisees which were from Jerusalem to Jesus saying why do you also transgress the commandment of God by your tradition? For God commanded saying Honor Your father and mother and he that curses his father or mother let him be put to death. (Matthew 15:1-4)

Jesus is saying that it is very important that the Jews honor their mother and father, but the Jewish scribes and Pharisees have made that commandment of none effect with their traditions.

"But you say, whoever says to his father and mother whatever is profit, is a gift to God...these people draw near to me with their mouth...teaching as doctrines the commands of men and honor me out of their mouth, but their heart is far from Me. Now that which goes into the mouth defiles a man, but that which comes out of the mouth this defiles him"

I'm stung by these words. "These people come near to me with their mouths, and honor me with their lips, but their heart is far from me, and in vain they worship me." I don't want to worship in vain, and I hope you don't either.

Examine your heart. Do you need to repent before God about your relationship with your mother and father? Have you used some kind of yardstick to determine whether or not you should honor them or revere them? Have you said, "Well, what ever good I did to you is a blessing to you. I don't owe you anything else." I would examine my heart, and I would see where I'm at with that, because only you and God know that.

The idea of this book on the Ten Commandments is that we get right with God in every way possible; that we examine our hearts; and that we allow the commandments of God, the precepts of God, to have their right place. Say to yourself if I'm failing, if I'm missing it, forgive me, I repent, and I want to get right with you.

Not that we manipulate the commandment and say that it doesn't count anymore because it's the Ten Commandments, I'm under grace, and I'm not under the law. You know what? That's lawlessness. Well, today the Lord desires to take time to explain to you that if you don't honor your mother and father, it is a sin. Christianity 101. But a lot of Christians leave that stuff behind, and they think they are going on to the deep things of God. They are worshiping in vain.

You've got to examine your heart. I believe in being honest. One thing that has brought me freedom and joy in my life is being honest with God. By keeping a pure heart, I have made this beatitude mine, "Blessed is He who has a pure heart, for they shall see God."

I want to see God, and not just in heaven. I believe I can see him here. He answers prayer. You can recognize Him just like Peter and say, "That's the Lord." You see the Spirit of God and know that God is moving in your life. Well maybe you've got to examine your heart. Maybe you've got to give mom a call, or write dad a letter. Maybe they are dead, and you've got to repent and forgive them.

If you let your kids get away with anything, you better repent before God. If you let them not respect you and not honor you, you've failed God there. They need to honor you. They need to respect you, because the Bible says they should and not because you are some tyrannical parent.

I recommend that you earn their respect and love. If that applies to you, ask the Lord to help you to give you a strategy, to show you how to bring about reconciliation with this Word of God. This is an important Word of God.

Maybe deep inside of you, you are angry that you've allowed them to not respect you, and that they do not honor you. You're mad on the inside. Guess what you are doing? You are holding back the blessing. You still have the power to say I approve of you, or I disapprove of you. And that kid is probably crying out and saying, "I really want them to like what I am doing." You've got to talk on a real honest level, the Word of God, not sports, the war, etc. Right now, you've got to deal with some stuff.

This is really important. It might not be the most exciting lesson you've learned, to honor your mother and father, but I want to tell you something: if you don't have it right, it is essential that you get it right. Through Jesus' death and resurrection, poor parent child relationships can be healed. There can be reconciliation. It can be brought into right relationship with God, and you can have tremendous joy. There is nothing like feeling like "Dad's proud of me" or giving your child honest approval.

I cherish the memory of my Dad's support of my ministry. When I had my little church for five years, guess who was my most faithful supporter? Every Wednesday night, every Sunday, my Dad was there. Rain or snow, it didn't matter. I knew he wasn't deep into the things in God. I knew that he was there because he was giving his approval. That was so important to me. And it is important that you honor your mother and father, to teach your children to honor you, and to make it easy for them to honor you and God at the same time by living your life fully for Jesus Christ.

6

Commandment #6:
Love Others;
Do Not Kill or Hate Them

Thou shalt not kill.
Exodus 20:13

You will show me the path of life. In your presence is
fulness of joy. At your right hand are pleasures
forevermore. (Ps: 16:11)

This scripture couldn't apply more to any of the
commandments than it does to murder, because what is the
opposite of the paths of life? Murder or death?

The sixth commandment does not literally mean you
shall not kill. The Hebrew really means that you shall not
take innocent life. Some people don't believe in capital
punishment and use this scripture to support their argument;
but the Bible doesn't teach this view at all. It's very plain
that the Bible teaches capital punishment.

So, let's look at this because we want to understand the
path of life. It's when we get outside of the path of life that
we experience the opposite of joy, which I believe is sorrow,
a heavy heart. God does not want us to have that. That's why
it's very important to understand a commandment such as
this. I believe it is very dear to the heart of the Lord.

How many people know that when you are in a state of
sin, you are not in a blessed position? You are not drinking
from the fountain; you are drying up; you are withering. It's
like ground that is parched, and it needs water, like a time of

refreshing. If you've ever seen a hot summer day and the ground and its cracks, think about your soul and the Holy Spirit raining on you, freshening up your heart. This commandment is especially for you, reader, if your heart has gotten hard, because we are going to go deeper into this idea of what it really means to "murder" someone.

What does it mean when the heart has conceived murder? What happens to your heart? Does it get dry and crusty? Does it need these times of refreshing in the presence of the Lord? Does it need for those sins to be blotted out, to break up that fallow ground, and for the rain of the Holy Spirit to come in and to refresh the ground?

I want to go deeper now. Let's look at what Paul says:

> For this, you shall not commit adultery, you shall not murder, you shall not steal, you shall not bear false witness, you shall not covet. If there is any other commandment, all are summed up in this saying, namely, you shall love your neighbor as yourself. Love does no harm to a neighbor; therefore, Love is the fulfillment of the Law. (Romans 13:9-10)

I explained to you in previous chapters how the Ten Commandments are broken into two sections. The first four commandments relate to loving God. The last six relate to loving our neighbor as ourselves. Along these lines, Paul says that if you love your neighbor, you will do him no harm; you won't murder him.

Now, why is it so important to have no murdering? The Bible says:

> Surely for your life blood I will demand a reckoning. From the hand of every beast I will require it, from the hand of man, from the hand of every man's brother I will require the life of a man. Whoever sheds man's blood, by man his blood shall be shed. For in the image of God He made man. (Genesis 9: 5-6)

The above scripture tells us why God requires that there will be no murdering – no taking of life – in His camp: because man is made in the image of God.

Why should there be an outcry against abortion? Because that is an innocent life created in the image of God. No murdering in the womb! The baby has a right to life. But why should it be okay to have capital punishment? Because in the same scripture it says "I will require the life of the man who sheds innocent blood." So, don't be confused by that. God is not the author of confusion. He is very clear and simple. It's man that makes it confusing.

It is because we are in the image and likeness of God that we do not have the right to kill that image and likeness. God created man. You cannot go in and destroy his life. God is the author of life, and I don't know how it happened and neither do scientists.

I have studied to a small degree the reproductive system in our bodies, and the understanding of the zygote, and the embryo, and the fetus, and then the newborn. What happens when the egg and sperm come together? I don't know, do scientists know – how life begins? Why when those two cells come together, does life begin? They don't know what has sparked life. And neither do you and neither do I; that's God's territory. It says the "unknown remains the unknown to God. The secret things belong to God" (Deut. 29:29). That's where we take it by faith. And we have to look at it with a little bit of awe and wonder and say, "Hey, that's God's business and I will not violate his plan of creation. That's just the way it happens."

Scientists can do amazing things nowadays, but they still don't know why or when life begins. But I tell you something – it begins when the egg and sperm unite and the egg is fertilized by the sperm. I taught on abortion and human growth and development. Just because a baby doesn't look like someone who is 90, we can't simply say that person is not human. Are they both not human? No, they are both human. You can't kill the old person with euthanasia and just say they don't count anymore because it is too expensive to care for them. You can't kill them! And you can't kill the baby in the womb at 9 months with the reasoning that, "Well, it's not really 2 years old and isn't independent. It still needs it's mother; and, therefore, it's still a parasite." That's what they call it, a parasite, because it's sucking its mother's life.

I will go all the way to conception, and ask is it a human even though that zygote doesn't look like a 21 year old? Yes, it is. God's life begins when that egg is fertilized. You should be strong with this people, because He said, "There will be no murdering in my camp." And you go ahead and be bold.

If you don't know what sin is, you cannot know what salvation is, especially in the case of murder. How can there be godly repentance and the blotting out of sin unless you are really able to say, "I have failed God, and I can't save myself – I need a savior." When you come to this revelation, there should be weeping. There should be visible signs of repentance. There should be true remorse. There should be an attitude that I'm going to go and change my life.

He has made it plain that some of our evangelistic strategies have failed, focusing only on the love of God. But when someone repents and says, "I have sinned. I have failed God. I need a savior and I'm not going to change. I need God to help me to walk this out. I need him on a daily basis because I can fail, and God is the strength of my life. I can't let go of that strength." You are going to stay with God because you need him every day. If there is not a true heart of repentance, you will be weakened.

So I want to take you deeper with this. I want to appeal to you. It also says in 1 Samuel that God's people can kill in war:

> Now go and attack Amelek and utterly destroy all that they have, do not spare them but kill both man and woman, infant nursing child, oxen, sheep, camel and donkey. (I Samuel 15:3)

When they went to war, they went to win under God's direction. If you are in a just war and you are a soldier, I believe you have the right to kill. Personally, I never wanted to do that. In fact, when I grew up during the Vietnam War era, I purposely went into nursing so that I could be a medic if called into service. I didn't want to dodge the draft, but I also didn't want to kill anyone.

But some people go to war and must kill others. Therefore, God needed to address this for the people of God. Regarding capital punishment, as I looked at that scripture, I began to understand the precepts of God. The Word of God is simple and plain. If someone is a serial killer and there is no repentance in them, there can be capital punishment – it is available to us, and it is scriptural. There are many examples in the Old Testament approving it.

Now, let's go deeper. I want to tell you more about this idea of understanding the law, understanding grace, and understanding this particular law of "Thou shalt not kill" (take innocent life). The first passage to look at is in the book of Matthew:

> Now behold, one came and said to him, "Good teacher, what good thing shall I do that I may inherit eternal life?" (Matthew 19:16)

This is a very important question, especially when we are trying to understand, "How do I go to heaven when I die?" I can hear myself asking this question to the Lord.

Jesus replied to him, "Why do you call me good? No one is good but one, and that is God (Matthew 19:27)." If you look at that a little deeper, Jesus was kind of playing with him. He wanted him to acknowledge that he was God. "Why do you call me 'good,' only God is good. Am I God?" Yes, he was.

Look at what he says, "If you want to enter into life, keep the commandments." He didn't say break the commandments and live by grace. He said to keep the commandments. This is basic, but it is good to hear.

Let's read on. He says, "Which one?" And Jesus says, "You shalt not murder." See, it doesn't say you shall not kill. No, it's murder – we're talking about taking innocent life. He continues:

"You shall not commit adultery, you shall not steal. You shall not lie. Honor your father and mother, and you shall love your neighbor as yourself." And the young man said to him, "All these things have kept." Jesus said, "if you want to be perfect, go and sell what you have, give to the poor and you will have treasure in heaven. You come and follow me." But the young man heard that saying, and he went away sorrowful for he had great possessions. And Jesus said to the disciples, "It is hard for a rich man to enter into the kingdom of heaven. And again I say, it is easier for a camel to go through the eye of a needle than for a rich man to enter the kingdom of God." And when his disciples heard it, they were greatly astonished and said, "Who then can be saved?" (Luke 18: 20-26)

This gives me the impression that they were rich. They had a problem with that. They must have had possessions. Stop and think for a moment. They thought, "Well, we didn't sell everything." So what is Jesus really saying? "He looked at them and said, 'With men, this is impossible. But with God all things are possible.'"

So what does Jesus want? Does he want legalistic obedience to the commandments? No. Does he want you to break the commandments? No, because he said keep the commandments. But the young man in his heart still knew, even though he had kept the commandments since a kid, that he still lacked something. Jesus hit the nail on the head and said sell everything you have and give it all away, and come and follow me. The man went away sorrowful. He is the only person in scripture who went away sorrowful after talking to Jesus. Everyone else went away leaping for joy, praising God for his healing; but this guy went away sorrowful.

And then Jesus said, "It's really hard for a rich man to enter heaven." Why? Because where is your heart? Jesus wanted to place that standard so high that the guy could not keep it. He wanted him to need God. He wanted to put him in a position of needing God, of being in a place of knowing that he can't do it on his own, but needing God's help. If any of you are out there and are trying to be religious and legalistic and controlling, then maybe God is telling you that's not enough – that you have got to need Him.

I think God must train us. But he has given me such a distaste for religion. I wanted to be free to worship God. I want to worship him not only in truth – they can have the greatest creed in the world, and all the doctrine written out – but I want to worship Him in spirit AND in truth. We've got to look at the spirit of the law, not the letter of the law. Now, let's see what Jesus said about murdering.

Now, we're ready to look at Matthew 5:21-26. "Jesus said, You have heard that it was said of old, You shall not murder." Does your translation say murder or kill? There's a difference here between killing and murdering. You can kill in self-defense, in war, and in capital punishment; but you can't kill innocent life, because that's called murder – no murder. Jesus said, "You've heard it said of old, You shall not murder, and whoever murders shall be in danger of the judgment." Now, those were Jews, and they knew the law. They knew that if they killed an innocent life, they would be killed. "But I say to you." This is Jesus bringing us to the place of understanding, the Spirit of this law. "I say to you, whoever is angry with his brother without a cause, shall be in danger of the judgment."

Now, come on. Read this here. Because some of you reading this chapter may have thought this one doesn't apply to me. Have you ever gotten angry with your brother without cause? You are in danger of the judgment. The Bible says, "Be angry, and sin not."

"Whoever says to his brother, 'Raca,'.." (this means "empty head") "...shall be in danger of the council, and whoever says, 'You fool,' shall be in danger of hell-fire."

Now, come on. Have you ever called someone a fool? Think about it, about you passing judgment because maybe they didn't treat the "wonderful" you right. How could that "empty headed fool" over there treat you wrong? Now, think about it. God wants to heal some of you reading this, because that anger is still inside of you. Did someone do such and such to you, and you're still mad at them? You've got a good memory. You can remember it all. You've gone over those details over and over again. How could they do that to YOU, and trespass against YOU, and trample over YOUR LIFE? You are thinking those fools, those empty headed fools. They didn't have a brain in their head that would make them treat you like that. And you think you've got every right to still hold on to this anger.

But let me tell you something more. Jesus says, "If you bring your gift to the altar, and there remember that your brother has something against you..." You come to church and are doing jumping jacks for Jesus. But inside, you are not right with God or with your brother. Do you know what Jesus says? "Leave your gift there and go your way. First be reconciled to your brother, and then come and offer your gift."

That's the spirit of "Thou shalt not murder!" Are you guilty of murder? Do you then have the audacity to come to the altar and praise God and act like some holy person? Or do you want to grow up in God and go to the next level, because you are not going to the next level until you get it right there? He will make you trample around the wilderness for another 40 years until you are ready to go to that next level. I know, because I've been there. You can't progress in God if you are holding that kind of anger in your heart.

Maybe you know someone who fell away from God. You think that they carried the biggest Bible in the church, and that person knew how to quote scripture. But they had bitterness in them. Then, you get around them and hear, "I don't' know what it is, but there's something not right with them." I've had that, talking to someone and feeling, "I can't put my finger on it, but the spirit isn't right there." And then all of a sudden, they start talking a little more to you. And you start getting to know them a little better. All of a sudden it begins to come out. It's like a consuming fire, and it will be there. It tries to come up to a surface, and you try to push it down. You aren't going to think about that. You aren't going to think about the person who hurt you. You aren't going to think about it. And there it comes back up.

Then, you get around someone spiritual and say, "I want to talk to you about something." They say, "Okay, let's talk." And then it comes up. I knew this one lady. She was divorced and was left with three children. In my own mind, I agreed with her. But her hatred for her ex-husband was consuming her. I told her, "You've got to let it go. It's killing YOU." She said, "You don't know what he did to me!" We were at the altar, and I just remember saying, "Wow, then I can't pray for you. We can't pray here. You've got to leave here, and go deal with it, and then you can come back." God can't forgive you if you don't forgive others. Now, let's look at what Jesus says here.

> Agree with your adversary quickly, while you are in the way with him, lest your adversary deliver you to the judge, and the judge hand you over to the officer, and you be thrown into prison. Assuredly, I say to you, you will by no means get out of there until you've paid the last penny. (Matthew 5:25-26)

Jesus is really serious about this. He says elsewhere, speaking to the Pharisees:

> But now you seek to kill me, a man who has told you the truth, which I've heard from God... (Abraham didn't do this)...You are of your father the devil. He was a murderer from the beginning, and does not stand in the truth because there is no truth in him. When he speaks a lie, he speaks from his own resources, for he is a liar and the father of it. (John 8:40, 44)

The devil is the author of murder. When you have hate in your heart, you are not acting like God, even though you are created in His image and likeness. That spirit is not of God. Don't try to say it's righteous anger. I know this personally.

There was a woman that I grew to hate over time. It built. It didn't happen quickly. I tried with all the spiritual resources that I thought that I had, but I really didn't surrender to God. I didn't take God's help into it. I kept thinking Frank is wonderful. She should be wonderful to him. Everyone else thinks he is wonderful. How come she doesn't? What's the matter with her? You know, all this kind of pride going on. And there was an incident, just before my dad died. I was weak, and I was tired. I was emotionally spent. I was spiritually low. Don't think the devil comes to you when you are strong. He comes after you've been fasting for 40 days and you are hungry. That's when he says, "Turn the stone into a piece of bread." It's when you are weak. That's why Jesus said the spirit is willing, the flesh is weak. The woman made a comment about my dad. I let her have it with both barrels. I felt justified. Guess who felt right? I was working at Henry Ford Hospital at the time. I thought I was really professional, but inside me there was this hate. I remember walking after that incident. I remember thinking in my heart that I hate her. Then I said this, "And I don't care what God says. I hate her."

Now, I'm telling you the truth. God then spoke to my heart in the ensuing days, and time passed. Now, I want to tell you something: there is no condemnation in this, not when He's talking to you. It's Hebrews 12. It's chastisement. It's good when your Father God chastens you when you have done wrong! It's good; it is not condemnation. Don't try to push it off saying there is therefore now no condemnation. Not when God's dealing with you, because He loves you as a Father. I had murder in my heart, and I want to tell you that I broke the 'thou shall not murder' commandment.

Maybe some of you have also been in a similar manner, by hating someone. God finally got me to a hearing place. I would come to church and praise the Lord and he would say, "What are you doing here? Leave your gift at your altar and go and reconcile with your brother, because your brother has something against you." I would come back to church the next Sunday and people would think, "Boy, isn't Frank spiritual?" Yeah, and God's telling me I don't belong in His house.

I am talking about growing up here. I am talking about really walking in love. I am talking about not getting away with "it," but allowing the Holy Spirit to really transform us. It's not about spiritual calisthenics; it really is about the heart. But out of a pure heart, you will have pure praise. I finally came to a place where God spoke to my heart, and I heard him. You know what he said to me? He said this is the worst sin you have ever committed. I've committed others, unfortunately, and I know God. That's why it's bad. It's worse when you know Him and you offend Him that way. The one who doesn't know Him as well is guilty of less stripes. I had to go through fire to get that thing burnt out of me, to get to that place of repentance. Then I had reconciliation and communication with the person and re-developed the relationship. God was able to reconcile it because I humbled myself and acknowledged that it was sin.

I had committed murder in my heart. The revelation of that broke my heart, and I didn't want to displease God like that. God forbid. I DO love God. But He says, "If you love me, you will keep my commandments." He didn't say if you love me, you'll live by grace. No, there is an obedience to the faith. Because of His grace, we love Him and we obey Him. If we hear Him say He's displeased when we displease Him, we need to be chastened by the Lord. I don't want that in my heart. Never again! I had to pull that root of bitterness up right from the root and throw that thing out. I had to commit to God my desire to show mercy, because he showed mercy to me.

I do love Jesus, and I grieve when I fail Him. But by His grace and by His strength, I'll never do that again. I learned a great lesson. I've learned something and am able to pass it onto you. I believe there is a demonic spirit of murder that can reside in the church kept hidden in the heart of the angry person.

If you feel that this is something that you need special prayers about, don't be ashamed. I look at it as the love of God compelling you to get right with him. If you feel that there is someone that you harbor hate towards – maybe an ex spouse, or a child or parent that has failed you, or someone that is dead, you need healing. God wants to work a work of healing in you through forgiveness of this sin. He will give you a fresh start.

7

Commandment #7:
Be Faithful, Not Adulterous

Thou shalt not commit adultery.
Exodus 20:14

There is a certain amount of added seriousness to this commandment. The others are all important and should be obeyed, but in this chapter we are talking about purity. In this section we're going to talk about sexual immorality, adultery from a sexual point of view, and also spiritual adultery.

I believe this shows us the path of life. In Proverbs it states over and over again, "Beware of the adulterous woman." "Don't go that way; go the other way." "Save your life; get out of there." "Flee sexual immorality. It leads to death and destruction."

In the chapters to come, we are going to talk about lying, stealing, and coveting, which really rates high. But, there is something about adultery that seems to be so clear in the scripture that one must take heed. You must be on guard and be sober and be vigilant, because it is easy to slip in this area. Even as we worship the Lord and stress His holiness, Christians that desire to be used by God in this hour must stress purity in their heart.

It is not a bondage to be holy. It is good to keep his commandments. It separates you. You are not saved by keeping them, because by faith you are saved through the grace of God; but He gives you the Holy Spirit to help you keep them. The Lord is sparing you problems by commanding you to stay pure.

You see, there is something that happens when you sin. The gentle dove of the Holy Spirit lifts up and moves. I don't believe you lose your salvation, but there is something about His presence. When you do something wrong, the spirit of God quickens inside you, whether it's in thought, word, or deed, and seems to lift and say, "I can't bless your work. I can't bless what you are doing." I'm not saying you will lose your salvation, but I want my life to be effectual in this generation, in this hour, and I hope that each and everyone of you do, too. It can't be without that close walk with God.

I'm learning more and more about a closer walk with God. Each day I desire to walk closely with Him. This is how you do it: repent, draw nigh unto Him, and allow Him to blot your sins and feel refreshed in the presence of the Lord. Even if you've committed adultery, there is forgiveness and healing for you.

But, Revelation 21:8 says, "The cowardly, the unbeliever, the abominable, the murderers, and the sexually immoral, sorcerers, idolaters, and all liars shall have their part in the lake of fire which burns with fire and brimstone, which is the second death." I was seeing here the obviousness of something, that for some reason, I didn't see before. The Lord God does want you to keep his commandments. If you don't keep his commandments, you don't love Him. "If you love me, you'll keep my commandments." If you are a liar, being sexually immoral, murdering and committing idolatry, if you do these things, where is your obedience to the faith and not to the law? Where is your obedience to the faith in Jesus Christ? He died for you. He wants you to be separated from sin and to be holy.

We're not talking about a law that can save you. We are talking about faith in Jesus Christ. I want you to think back to the cross and the red blood streaming down – that was an altar, and that blood was shed for us for our salvation. We must have faith in the blood for the forgiveness of our sins.

Some people are twisted into thinking that they can do their own things, and that it's okay. I believe there has to be an obedience to the faith. I believe the Lord is talking about grace on this subject and not the law. You have to know that you can't be pure without the blood of Jesus. You can't keep the law. That is why you can't be saved by the law; it's a heart thing. You have to know that the blood has been shed, and the sacrifice has been made. It is made available for you to walk in this.

Let's say that you do fall into sin. The good man rises back up again. If we sin, we have an advocate with the Father. But you've got to know the heart of God in order to know the heart of the true Christian. Look at Hebrews 1:9, "You have loved righteousness, and hated lawlessness." I want to emphasize that God HATES lawlessness. If you think you can be a Christian and you are doing your own thing in sin, I say Wake up! Wake up to righteousness, and sin not the Bible says. The author of Hebrews is commending Jesus here, saying, "You have loved righteousness and hated lawlessness, therefore God, your God, has anointed you with the oil of gladness more than your companions."

I would like to say something to you regarding this idea of sexual immorality. You will not know joy if you are living in sin. You will not know the oil of gladness if you are full of fantasy, lust, pornography and all kinds of sexual immorality going on inside of you. Maybe you haven't completed the actual act of adultery, but you are allowing all of that garbage and lust inside of you. You are not going to know joy. You are going to know depression. You are going to know unhappiness. God wants you to have joy – the joy of the Lord is your strength. It's not about how much sin you can get by with and still be saved. I think it's about being strong in the Lord.

I don't want to just endure my walk with God; I want to enjoy this. God wants us to enjoy the ride. He wants you to have joy unspeakable and full of glory. He wants you to have the oil of gladness above your fellows. And if you don't have that, it's okay for you to ask yourself to check your heart and say, hey, wait a minute. God even says I can have joy in the midst of trial. He wants you to have joy even when times aren't so perfect, because your joy is in the Lord. But if you are in sin, you won't have joy in the Lord. Maybe you walk through the motions and you live out the life, but there isn't the joy. But to obey from the heart of purity is God's will.

Let's focus on adultery. What does the word adultery mean? In Greek and Latin, it means to "alter" something. The adulteration of something makes it impure. When something is adulterated, it is not clean any more. They adulterated it. They made it impure. Something other than the pure thing has stepped in and made it unclean. Dirty. That is the adulteration of a thing; it is no longer clean.

That is what happens in a marriage when adultery occurs. The other thing steps in and it is no longer a pure covenant. It really has to do with this idea of holiness and holiness in your mind, body, and heart. I want to look at the words of Jesus, and then the words of Paul. Jesus affirms the commandment of Exodus 20:14: "You shall not commit adultery." He said,

> You have heard how it was said of old, "you shall not commit adultery." But I say to you, whoever looks at a woman to lust for her, he has already committed adultery with her in his heart. (Matthew 5:27-28)

He didn't say go ahead and commit adultery, because you are under grace. No, He didn't say that. What are you lusting after with the heart? Jesus meant business; he meant what he said. It wasn't a casual reference. Jesus also said:

> If your right eye causes you to sin, pluck it out and cast it from you. It's more profitable for you that one of your members perish than that your whole body was cast into hell. And if your right hand causes you to sin, cut it off, and cast it from you. It is more profitable for you that one of your members perish

70

than that your whole body be cast into hell. (Matthew 5:29-30)

I want you to think about this. He does not want you to pluck out your eye or cut off your hand. He wants to get your attention! He wants you to hear this, to say, "I really mean what I am saying here!" You can't fill your eyes with lust and your heart with lust and still expect to go to heaven.

I didn't say it, Jesus said it. He said you will go to hell if you allow yourself to do that. Better for you to pluck your eyes out than for you to go to hell. But you might say, "I'm saved by grace. I can do anything."

Well, I don't know. I wouldn't want to base my eternity on that. I would want to have a repentant heart so that times of refreshing can come from the presence of the Lord. If I got into that, I want to say, "Look I'm sorry, I missed it here. Lord, please forgive me. I want to be clean and holy and to do your will. This is not just about me having illegal pleasures in this life." No, He said if you love me, if you want to be my disciple, you will take up your cross, deny yourself, and follow me. Yes, there is self-denial in the Christian walk. Does it mean He doesn't want to prosper you and bless you and heal you? No. I believe in blessings, and healing and prosperity in God; but not if you are not walking in His commandments. That is the will of God. In Proverbs and Deuteronomy, it says "If you don't walk in the blessings, you are going to walk in the curses." We've got to have the wisdom of God. We've got to love wisdom. With all your wisdom, get wise, wake up!

Some will say, "I think Jesus died on the cross for my sins, and I can do anything I want because I'm under grace." To this I respond that I too believe His grace is immeasurable, and I thank God for His grace. I wouldn't be writing this without his grace. But repentance is the way to grace, and God cares what happens inside the heart. He judges the heart. The Bible says, "Only the spirit of the man can know the spirit that is inside of him." I believe only God

71

can know what is the spirit of a man – what is inside your heart. I can't read your heart, but God can.

This is why there are such spiritual implications when we are talking about adultery, because He likens spiritual adultery to natural adultery. When we look at the covenant between the husband and the wife, and what happens when that covenant is broken, you will understand when you break covenant with God why it is called "spiritual adultery."

Are you lusting after some other thing instead of God? Are you filled with idolatry, pride, arrogance, "you and wonderful you," or is it about loving the presence of the Lord and wanting to be with Jesus, and understanding the crucifixion, the resurrection, the salvation, and the eternal implications?

See, when it's a matter of the heart, you can look good and look religious, but still really love the world. He who loves the world is at enmity with God – separated from Him. "He who is a friend of the world is an enemy of God." This is Bible! God wants you to be pure in your relationship with him. If you have been committing spiritual adultery, today is the day to repent. Today is the day to receive refreshing from the presence of the Lord and to recommit yourself to the Lord. You should renew your vows to the Lord.

But if you have broken covenant with Him and have said, "I don't want to really love you. I'm thinking about the world. I want to really make it in the world and go and fulfill the lusts of my flesh (money, fame, fortune, etc.)," it would be like a married man looking lustfully upon another woman, because you are the spiritual bride of Christ.

Wouldn't it be wrong for me to want another woman when I'm married to different woman? If I were to lust after her in my heart, that would be so wrong. We have to think about that in our relationship with God. When we love God so much with a pure heart, isn't it adulterous to say, "I want the world. I want the things of the world"? I think we all get caught up with that, just as it is easy to lust with our eyes and to look at the attractions of the world. That's why we have to keep our hearts pure.

I'm not saying you will lose your salvation over this. But what I am saying is, in order to be a strong Christian, you have to repent of this. You have to turn away from this 180 degrees. You will receive times of refreshing from the presence of the Lord. You will have the joy of the Lord, the oil of gladness; then you are strong in Him and can really be who He called you to be. Now, let's look at it from Paul's point of view.

> Food is for the stomach and the stomach for food. But God will destroy both it and them. Now the body is not for sexual immorality, but for the Lord. And the Lord for the body....1 Corinthians 6:13

> And God both raised up the Lord, and He'll also raise us up with his power. Do you not know that your bodies are members of Christ? Shall I then take the members of Christ and make them members of a harlot? (1 Corinthians 6 14-15)

Now, there is some kind of connection between God and our body. Your bodies are temples of the Holy Spirit. So, of course, you should not take the members of Christ (your body) and make them members of a harlot! Certainly not! Are you going to drag Jesus into your sin? When you do that, you are bringing the Holy Ghost, the spirit who dwells in you, into your sin. Paul would say God forbid.

Read what Paul also says, "Do you not know that he who is joined to a harlot is one body with her?" When you connect with someone who is not your spouse and commit adultery, you are joined to that person as if you are married to them. God wants to reveal truth, so that truth sets you free.

Paul continues, "For the two shall become one flesh." If you have multiple partners, it is like you have multiple marriages.

"But he who is joined to the Lord is one spirit with Him." He is likening the marriage covenant between a man and a woman with the marriage covenant between God and

His people. Flee sexual immorality; don't entertain it, flee from it. Flee, he says.

"Every sin that a man does is outside of his body, but he who commits sexual immorality sins against his own body." Don't you tell me every sin is equal, and every sin is alike, that "sin is sin." That's not what my Bible says. This sin affects you in a different way. You drag Christ through the mud when you commit adultery and fornication, and sit and look at that pornography, and absorb that evil, lustful spirit into you. He says every other sin is outside of the body, but "Do you not know that your body is the Temple of the Holy Spirit who is in you who you have from God, and that you are not your own?"

You gave Him your life, isn't that the deal? Or did you give Him only part of it? I thought the commitment was "I give my life to you, Lord." That's everything, that includes the body. The Bible says, "you have been bought with a price; therefore, glorify God in your body." And what are you going to do with that. Are you going to be a good steward of your body? Look at what He says in Ephesians, in this context of the Ten Commandments:

> Thou shalt not commit adultery. Wives, submit to your own husbands as to the Lord. The husband is the head of the wife as Christ is the head of the church. He is the Savior of the body. Therefore, just as the church is subject to Christ, let the wives be subject to her husband in everything. Husbands love your wife just as Christ loved the church and gave Himself for her, that He might sanctify and cleanse her with the washing of the water by the Word. That He might present her to Himself, a glorious church, not having spot or wrinkle or any such thing, that she should be holy and without blemish. (Ephesians 5:22-27)

That's our call. That's what we have to do if we want Christ to come. So husbands are to love their wives as their own bodies. He who loves his wife, loves himself. They became one flesh.

For no one ever hated his own flesh, but nourishes it and cherishes it, just as the Lord does the church. For we are members of his body, and of his flesh, and of his bone. For this reason a man shall leave his father and his mother and join to his wife, and the two shall become one flesh. This is a great mystery, but I'm speaking concerning Christ and the church. Nevertheless, let each one of you in particular, so love his own wife as his self, and let the wife see that she respects her husband. (Ephesians 5:29-33)

This is a great mystery; and I'm not going to pretend to tell you that I understand it all. But what I do understand, I desire to convey to you with all my heart. I would say there are warning signals. There are flashing lights saying, "Don't go that way. It's a lie; it's destructive. There are blessings on the other route." And I would say to you now, along with Jeremiah the prophet, who says, "For of old, I have broken your yoke and burst your bonds. And you said, I will not transgress, when on every high hill and on every green tree, you lay down, playing the harlot. O generation, they say, 'If a man divorces his wife and goes from him, and becomes another man's, may he return to her again?' Would not that land be greatly polluted? But you have played the harlot with many harlots."

And yet, is this our relationship with the Lord? "Oh, I love Jesus, but the world has got this thing going on right now." "I love God, and He died for me, but I'll put God on the shelf right now while I pursue my career." Is that not pollution? He says that is what Israel did. They served God when it was convenient. That's what He called playing the harlot. That's what he called spiritual adultery, having many lovers, and yet you are married with somebody else.

This message really spoke to my heart, because I want to be pure. In my heart, I want to go deeper. In my heart, I want you to go deeper. I'm asking you with me to renew our vows to the Lord. Let's really give him our heart, just like you gave your husband or wife your heart when you married them.

You had every intention of just loving them, and they were so wonderful. Then something happened and you had a big fight, and you slept on the couch. Go in and make up rather than letting the sun set on your anger. There is forgiveness and healing in the marital relationship.

The same is true in our marriage relationship with the Lord. We haven't arrived yet. That's what the Ten Commandments are about. They show us reality, and that we cannot keep them. It is such a paradox, because it shows us our iniquity. Paul says, "I would not know coveting was a sin unless I heard the law say 'Thou shalt not covet.' And I will not know adultery had I not heard the word."

So I don't want anyone to get under condemnation, because that would be wrong. We are not studying the law to understand condemnation. We are studying the law that it would drive us to say, "I want to be purer. I want to be holier. I want to be more sanctified, more set apart." Get your heart right with God. If you should fail, get right back up again and be cleansed through faith in the blood of Jesus.

Don't be afraid to share this with the world, because this is the message of God. Some may weep at your kitchen table, because they have failed. But it is okay for them to know sin that they might know their Savior, that they might know so great a salvation. A great price was paid because we could not keep the law. We've got to desire purity, but always appreciate the blood that was shed for us to cleanse our impurities.

8

Commandment #8:
Be a Giver, Not a Taker

Thou shalt not steal.
Exodus 20:15

This commandment was one of those spoken by God, very abruptly, from the mountain: No stealing! He spoke it out with the authority of a command. He didn't want this going on among his people. I believe the Lord would want us thinking on this – if you keep nine commandments but break one, you are still a lawbreaker.

When you look at these commandments, you know that we need a savior. We needed Jesus to die for us. As we've looked at each of these commandments, I've realized that I've broken all of them, in terms of the "spirit" of the command.

Maybe you insist, "I don't steal." Well, let's see. What is God saying? What is it like to have a pure heart when it comes to stealing? What is it that you steal that maybe someone else doesn't steal? Maybe you have a way of taking what isn't yours. Maybe you have stolen someone's self-worth.

And the peace of God which surpasses all understanding will guard your heart and mind in Christ Jesus. (Philippians 4:7)

To be in the presence of God is to have this peace of God which passes all understanding. God will give you joy and peace. If you have ever stolen anything, you come to the conclusion that this is one way to lose peace. You are worried about being found out and caught. Some people get a rush out of stealing, even movie stars – out of taking something that isn't theirs. But the best way to lose peace is to take something that isn't yours, to take something that belongs to someone else.

Stealing becomes a pattern of how you act. So if you start down the road of taking things (e.g., taking a box of pens from work or cheating on your income taxes), this idea can build up inside of you without you even realizing it. Then you become like the devil, because he has been a thief from the beginning. You should want to act like Jesus – Jesus doesn't take what doesn't belong to Him. That's why he was so mad with the one man that hid the talent in the ground who said of God, "You take what doesn't belong to you." God was angry with that. That was an accusation against his character that was not true. God doesn't take what doesn't belong to him.

God is not a thief. He will not take your blessing away. You don't have to be afraid of God swooping down and stealing your blessing from you. I believe you will lose it if you are living in disobedience, pride, unbelief. Yes, God will see your unbelief and take it from you and give it to someone who does have belief.

God is a blesser. He says no stealing. If he tells you to not steal, do you think he will then steal from you? How can you trust in a thief? God is not a thief. He will give you good measure, pressed down, overflowing, because you have trusted in him. But if you steal, you will be stolen from, I promise you, because you will reap what you have done.

God wants to bless you, but he will not bless a thief. If you want to get on the blessing path, you need to get right. No more ripping people off and claiming that God understands. God understands that you are a thief. Paul was speaking to Ephesians when he said don't steal anymore. He was talking to Christians. Christians are under grace, but they don't have the right to steal.

This basic Word of God gives you peace if you will obey it. Don't take something unless you ask if you can have it. If you will walk above reproach, I believe God will bless you.

If you go and steal and do not function to the perfection which God has called you to function, the whole body will suffer. God doesn't want that and neither do you.

I want to show you something. When God says don't steal, what he is saying in the positive is that you can own possessions. It's okay to own private property. God is saying you can own; I will entrust you with property. I will grant you the power to possess things, and I don't want your things stolen. Don't listen to the cults that tell you that you must live in poverty and not own anything, and must take the vow of poverty. But there is another side of this: two conditions to owning things.

> Hear this you cows of Bashan....who oppress the poor... (Amos 4:1)

You cannot have possessions at the expense of the poor. You cannot climb the ladder of success at the expense of other people. You cannot take from the poor and give to yourself. Elsewhere, in Amos He says,

> ...who drink wine from bowls...and are not grieved at the afflictions of Joseph. (Amos 6:6)

What he is saying here is that you must have compassion for others, and the poor, in your prosperity. God is telling you that you can have possessions, but you must visibly care for others.

The most important thing with God is LIFE. God honors life. He came to give us life. There is the sanctity of life. How do you put this together with this command to not steal? When you go to work every day and work hard, at the end of 40 hours, they present you with a check and say, "This represents your life's work; you have worked for this.

You have given of your life, and we give you a monetary value of your life." So what you own determines what is important to you, what you have labored for, what you have obtained through your labor and your life. God respects life, and he doesn't want someone to come in to your house and steal your TV or VCR, or possessions, because you have given life for those things. What you labor for is important to you, and it's important to God.

Are your priorities in order? You must examine yourself and answer that question between you and God. But if you seek first the kingdom of God and His righteousness, all these things will be added to you.

What does he say in Malachi that really hurts him?

> Will a man rob God?...You have robbed me in your tithes and offerings. (Malachi 3:8-10)

Do you see that you can be a thief and steal what belongs to God. He asks are you a thief and withholding from God? What do you do with your labor and your life and your struggles? Hopefully, you help those in need. What does God do with the tithe? He says to bring all the tithes in the storehouse that there may be food in my house. He wants to provide food with that tithe. He wants to feed people. But if you don't learn to trust God and tithe and give to Him, then you are robbing from God and robbing from others who God wants to feed, both physically and spiritually.

I want you to read something that really opened up the rationale about not stealing to me. In the book of Ephesians, the Bible says:

> Let him who stole, steal no longer, but let him labor for what is good that he may have something to give to him who is in need. (Ephesians 4:28)

Why do you get that paycheck? Is it to only expend on yourself, to meet your needs and pleasures? What are you wasting your life on? Are you wasting your life on the things that will perish and waste away?

I love Psalms 41 which says:

Blessed is he who considers the poor; The Lord will deliver him in time of trouble. The Lord will preserve him and keep him alive, And he will be blessed on the earth; You will not deliver him to the will of his enemies. The Lord will strengthen him on his bed of illness; You will sustain him on his sickbed. (Psalms 41:1-3)

Your enemies may be thorns, but God will give you the victory if you will help the poor and if you will quit stealing, and say the Lord deserves His tithe. There are spiritual and other needs the church must meet.

Look at your neighbor and say I will not rob from them or cheat them. At work, you want to work for 40 hours to get paid for 40 hours, and God will bless you. If you have been stealing but now will repent before the Lord, something will rise up within you and you will be redeemed. God will promote you.

God has dealt with me. There are always ways to cut corners and not give God 100%. But God cares about the details. I am an "employee of the Lord" and won the "Employee of the Year" award last year. Promotion comes from the Lord in every area of life. If you humble yourself, God will exalt you. If you walk in the honor and integrity of God, God will exalt you and prosper you and lift you up. But if you are thief, no matter how much you are involved in missions and other areas, you will not be blessed.

Let's go to the heart of Jesus here. In Acts 20:35, Paul says, "I have shown you in every way, by laboring like this, that you must support the weak." We have got to give to those in need. It is not an option as a believer. Paul says, "Remember the words of the Lord Jesus that it is more blessed to give than to receive." This is the very heart of this message. Are you a taker or a giver? Is it all about you?

What can YOU get out of it? Are you a taker? Are you always out for YOU? You see, it is more blessed to give than to receive.

Of course, we all have needs. There are times when your soul has legitimate needs – your mind, your will, your emotions. We are a three-part being. We have physical needs. If I don't eat, I will get sick. If I don't rest, I will be tired. And your soul must be tended to as well. Your spirit must be fed as well. You must walk in the way of the Lord. As you allow your three-part being to be ministered to, you will know by the spirit when those times come that you must lay aside your desire and allow someone else's needs to be met. That's when you prefer someone above yourself. You know by the Spirit of God when you get into that situation. Are you a taker or are you a giver?

This is where thievery in the spirit-realm occurs. You are taking something that does not belong to you, in the spirit This is the worst kind of stealing there can be. You hinder the move of the Holy Spirit. If you will yield at that point and say, "I will give," "I will surrender," you will open the door to the spirit in your life, to blessing in your life. It is more blessed to give than to receive because God will defend you, God will exalt you, God will promote you. But if you disobey the Spirit and do not give when God calls you to, you will miss the blessings of the Lord.

Now is the time for you to examine your heart and say, "I will not steal any longer what belongs to someone else. I will not try to take their place. I will not push them out of the way and promote myself. I am going to let the Lord exalt me, and show me what He wants me to do. I will be content with the things I already have."

I guarantee you, the Lord will show you His pleasure. There is nothing like hearing the Lord saying, "This is my beloved son, in whom I am well pleased." Do not steal from anybody. If you take something that is not yours, you will have to walk that circle and give it back before you can move on and experience God's true blessings.

If you will release it to God, and say, "I know that you want to give me things, and you will protect my things." If you can trust in the Lord, He will trust you with eternal riches. He will exalt and promote you and use you. You will experience His good pleasure.

I want to close this chapter with a scripture:

> We then who are strong ought to bear the weaknesses of the weak, and not to please ourselves. Let each of us please his neighbor, for his good, leading to his edification. For even Christ did not please himself, but as it is written, "The reproaches of those who reproached you fell on me." (Romans 15:1-3)

This is so hard to live out. I'm not saying this is easy – the natural inclination of our flesh is to please ourselves. But Jesus is our example. Christ didn't try to please himself and neither should we. It is about lifting up and edifying the body of Christ.

I received a letter from someone whose mother I visited in the hospital. You don't know what you mean to somebody when you do something for somebody else. I didn't know what it meant to this mother and her daughter. I didn't feel like going to the hospital either, but I knew that I had to go. We do things out of obedience and not out of the flesh realm. The mother did end up dying, but I prayed with her in that hospital room. After praying for her, the mother told her daughter, "When I get better, I want to go to that church." She said she felt she would find the family she was looking for. In giving to her, I helped her find peace. It gave me great joy in return.

9

Commandment #9:
Honesty is the Best Policy:
Take It from God

Thou shalt not bear false witness against thy neighbour.
Exodus 20:16

This commandment I found to be very interesting, because it deals with the idea of witnessing against someone in a trial or court setting. But there is also the greater explanation of thou shalt not lie, and we see that in Ephesians 4:25. Paul was writing to Christians and telling them to put away lying: "Put away all lying and let each of you speak truth..." Elsewhere, the Bible says:

> Whoever keeps his (God's) word, truly the love of
> God is perfected in him....ought himself also to walk,
> just as he walked. (1 John 2:5-6)

Does that mean you can be a profuse liar, because Jesus was a liar? No, Jesus was truth. We will understand why it is essential for the Christian to not lie and to put away lying from them. They must walk as Jesus walked.

Today is the day for you to become pruned, to put away lying from your life – even little white lies. He wants you to be holy and pure and to walk as He walked. Jesus didn't tell white lies or any other kind of lies. We obey the Lord because He died for us. The Holy Spirit has been given to us. We have an opportunity to be more like God. We, in the Spirit, press on toward the prize because of the blood of

Jesus which cleanses us from unrighteousness. There must be a sincere desire on our part to obey God and follow His example and commands. Since He spoke truths, we must speak truth.

I want to emphasize to you the idea of understanding truth. The Bible says:

> There are six things the Lord hates, yes seven that are an abomination to Him...[One of them is] A false witness who speaks lies. (Proverbs 6:16, 19)

God hates a false witness. It is an abomination to Him. If you are caught in the idea, "Well, it really doesn't matter," you must know it DOES matter to God. In James, the Bible says, "the tongue is like a rutter which can direct a ship." Your tongue can direct the whole course of your life, and yet it is very hard to control. If this is such a huge negative, that God hates a false witness – someone who lies – then I want you to know that the reverse is also true. God loves a truthful witness. God loves when you walk in the truth. God wants you to understand this.

We are going to look at the positive, but we must understand the negative. We must grow in this passion to know truth and to walk in truth. We must understand the reverse, the detestable, the thing that God hates, and why He hates falsehood, pretense, when we put on airs, and when we stir up strife among the brethren by saying things bad about people.

Why does God hate that? Let's look at the book of Isaiah to answer that. Isaiah spoke to the people of Israel, and it applies even more to us:

> You are my witnesses, saith the Lord. (Isaiah 43:10-13)

That's why: because you are his witness, and you can't be a false witness for God. You can't be a lying witness or speak out of both sides of the mouth. You've got to speak truth to your neighbor in love. He continues:

> You are my witnesses and my servants who I have
> chosen that you may know and believe me.
> (Isaiah 43:10-13)

Now, what does it mean to know and believe God? How do you really witness for the Lord. I want to talk to you about your testimony. You've got a testimony and it is something more than the day you came and knelt at the altar, accepted Jesus Christ, and got saved. You are walking in your testimony every day. You've got to be walking in truth.

The root word in "testimony" is "test." You will be tested in your faith. You will be tested as a witness for Jesus Christ. They will examine you and look you up and down to see if you are for real. If you are for real, you will pass the test. Your testimony will be enhanced. You will be given more power, more privilege in the Lord. He will exalt you when you know the truth and walk in the truth. But if you have a lying tongue, he will not use you.

God has a way of being present to us and speaking to us. God is dealing with all of us as Christians, that we must watch our tongue. It is not okay to say some things a little "off-color." This issue is important to God. Too much humor (coarse jesting) could really hurt someone spiritually.

We have to watch, be sober, be vigilant, and be alert. We want our prayers answered. We want the presence and move of God. If we want to be in the presence of a holy God, there is an obedience required. You might say, "Hey, if someone talks about me, then I'll talk about them." God wants you to get out of that carnal place and into that spiritual place. He wants you to find time in His Word, to grow in the spirit and to hear his Word. He wants to fill you with truth. You've got to ensure that fresh water and salty water don't come out of your mouth, only truth. He says that we are His chosen ones. If we will obey Him even in the little things, He wants to bless us and put us in a place of influence. He goes on to say:

...that you may know and believe me, and understand that I am He, that before me there was no God formed, that besides me there is no savior. I have proclaimed that there is no foreign God among you; therefore you are my witnesses, says the Lord, that I am God....I work and who will reverse it? (Isaiah 43:10-13)

Do you understand that we are his witnesses that He is God? Now look at Isaiah 44:

Do not fear or be afraid. Have I not told you and declared it that you are my witnesses. Is there a god beside me? Indeed there is none; I am the one. (Isaiah 44:8)

The object of our witness, the object of our testimony, what we are testifying to, is that He is God. We are testifying to the fact that Jesus did die, that Jesus did rise, that His resurrection power makes a difference in our life. We are a testimony that He is God and that there is none other besides Him. That is what our life is all about. According to that standard, you are his representative in the earth. You are His witness. God forbid that you be a false witness or a tainted witness. God forbid that you should not stand up in a court of law and be able to bear true witness. Let it not be said of you by the Lord, "No I don't want that one taking the stand, they are a false witness." Let that never be said about you. You be the prime witness that He is God, He is alive, and He is at work in the earth.

That's the truth – that's what it means to be a witness. You are witnessing to the fact that Jesus Christ is alive. There is a witness in you. It's not about you getting a prayer answered. Rather you are testifying to the mighty nature of God. Your life counts for the Lord. You are important to His plan. God wants you to understand why you cannot be a liar, why you can't shade the truth and make yourself look good when it's not true. Jesus said this:

Pilot therefore said to him, "Are you a king?" Jesus answered "...for this cause was I born...come into the world...that I should bear witness to the truth. Everyone who is of the truth hears my voice. (John 19:37)

This is Jesus' mission statement. For you who work in the corporate world or who work in the church – we have mission statements. What is our purpose? This is Jesus' mission statement: "for this purpose I came into the world to bear witness of the truth." That's why He came! His life would bear up under the test. His would be a true testimony. So must yours.

Our testimony should be this: that there is no other way to get to God but through Jesus Christ. That's the truth. He said, "I am the way, the truth, and the life." That is the final reality, not some facade that looks like truth. Jesus is the truth. Some may not say that He is the King of Kings or the Lord of Lords, but he is. That's the truth; that's the final reality. You can base your life on that. You can testify, you can witness, you can even be a martyr. That's what the word "witness" really means – martyr. We can be a witness for Jesus, even unto death.

It is only when we come to this basic level of understanding, to get a mission statement for your life, to know what you your life is about, that you can really testify in truth about Jesus. Jesus said, "I came to bear witness of the truth." Do you know the truth? Now, I have to tell you something here. If you are a liar and if you practice lying, you better be quick to repent. If you've been lying and slandering and talking gossip about people, you must repent.

The reason God doesn't like these things is because it hurts people. People are created into His glorious image and likeness. So when you are hurting them, you are hurting Him. The Bible says, "How can you love God and hate your brother?" In John 8:44, He says, "You are of your father the devil, and the desires of your father, you want to do." The devil was a liar from the beginning and he does not stand in the truth. Because there is no truth found in Him. There is no truth in the devil. It's all a lie. It's all smoke and mirrors. Anything that he is tempting you with, that is not in line with the Word of God, is bad. It is not truth or freedom. It is bondage. The devil is a liar and the father of lies. He births lies into the earth. When you look at something that is contrary to the Word of God, it is born of Satan.

If God says something is a sin, then it is a sin. If you have gotten in the trap of believing a lie that says sin is not sin, that is a lie and you are in bondage and you must get out of it. That is a false witness. You don't have to be in oppression and depression, God wants to loose you and set you free. God has a plan for your life. You can know the truth, and the truth will make you free. Whatever your situation is, today is the day of salvation for you. Deliverance has come. That is why God is a God of truth, because Jesus came to set the captives free. He came to bring truth. He came to set the standard. The truth will set you free. The Bible says,

> I rejoice greatly that I have found some of your children walking in the truth, as we have received commandment from the Father. (3 John 4)

God rejoices when we see someone walking in the truth. When someone is walking in the truth of their calling in God, He rejoices. God wants us to understand the truth that He has for each and every one of us. The Bible also says:

> He who believes in the Son of God has the witness in himself. He who does not believe God has made him a liar because he has not believed the testimony that God has given in his Son. (1 John 5:10)

When someone will bold-facedly look at you and say, "I don't believe Jesus is God...maybe he was a prophet or a good teacher," they are saying God is a liar, because God's testimony is that Jesus is His Son. They can't pick and choose scriptures to believe and doubt others. You have to understand this testimony. The father spoke to Jesus, Jesus spoke to the apostles, and the apostles wrote it down. We have the Word of God. We have the word of truth. When they say, "I don't believe it," then they are calling God a liar and calling him the devil, the father of lies. That is what Satan is, and there is no truth in him. Something should rise up in you. Something should tell you to speak out and speak the truth in love, to speak the truth to someone because you love them and want to speak truth into their heart.

You must live in the Word of God. You must allow the Word of God to live in you in truth. It is the bread of life and comes inside of you and feeds the spirit-man. You become the Word made flesh, like Jesus. Jesus is the truth. The Word becomes flesh in you when you feed on it, day in and day out. To the degree that you know the Word of God, the truth, and act on it is the degree to which you know and follow Jesus. The Word of God must live in and through you, so your reactions are based on the Word of God, not on the flesh, circumstances, or on lies. Then people will see Jesus in you. It is a natural flow.

We will close this chapter with a prayer by Jesus in the Bible. I'd like you to put this scripture to memory. Jesus prayed this prayer before he went to the cross.

Sanctify them by your truth. Your word is truth.
(John 17:17)

I pray that prayer. Father, sanctify me by your truth. Your word is truth. Father set me apart by your truth; make me who you want me to be, when you want me to be it.

It is only by the separating action that the Word causes, that we will please God and give true witness to Him. That is why no lying should occur in the Christian.

10

Commandment #10:
Meaning it When You Say,
"God Bless You"

Thou shalt not covet *thy neighbour's house, thou shalt not covet thy neighbour's wife, nor his manservant, nor his maidservant, nor his ox, nor his ass, nor any thing that is thy neighbour's.*
Exodus 20:17

In previous chapters, we've talked about sex, violence, and murder. In this chapter, we talk about greed. Sex, murder, violence, and greed – God knows where it's at. He knows what's happening; we can't fool God. He knows how to handle your situation, what the right words are to say, and how to help you get right with Him.

As I meditated on this 10th commandment of not coveting, it is one of the most powerful of the Ten Commandments. God saved it for last; and, in a way, it ties all of the commandments together.

Covetousness is when you want someone else's things. It's a matter of the heart. Some people think that covetousness is not as bad as stealing, because it never comes to fruition. But I want to say that covetousness has caused more misery in lives than something that someone has stolen. It is an outright thing when someone steals, but covetousness is very much under the covers, very much kept secret. It is passive-aggressive behavior. Someone is out to get you, and they don't want you to know about it. It's a heart kind of thing. It's on the inside. God wants to examine your heart today because God wants to bless you. He will not bless the covetous individual. If you are covetous, you are an idolater.

We are all guilty of this; no one is above it. The sad thing is that we can't keep this commandment. It is like a slithering snake that slips inside you without you even realizing it. The key to overcoming is weeding your garden every day. Get that thing out of your heart. Do not let a root of bitterness spring up inside of you. Do you want to always look at someone else's life? They've got more education, more money, more humility...anything you can be covetous about. It's really a heart thing. Remember, you are a member of the body of Christ, and you have special gifts and skills that God has given you. If you have that negative attitude of covetousness towards someone else's blessings, then you tie God's hands.

If you are always thinking that you will never measure up, that someone else is better than you, then you will never soar. You will never ride the high places. He wants you to scale the mountains. Don't let anyone rain on your parade and say, "Not you, you're not good enough." There will be many who will bring you down. Even Jesus' neighbors in his hometown did not think He could possibly be the Son of God. Go ahead and be different. Go ahead and step outside of that mold and be someone great.

I'm going to show you something that if you understand this, you'll understand the whole teaching. The Bible tells us that Jesus was crucified because of covetousness:

> Pilate answered them, "do you want me to release to them the King of Jews?" because he knew that the chief priests had handed him over because of the envy in their heart. " (Mark 15:9-10)

Pilate was smart. He knew that the chief priests wanted to have what Jesus had. They wanted to be the ones that made the blind to see. They wanted to be the ones that had all the crowds clamoring after them, instead of standing by the sidelines and being rebuked by Him because of their religion.

94

Don't ever get caught on the sidelines of where the action is; instead, go to where God's spirit is moving. Don't wait for perfection; get involved now. There is nothing perfect this side of heaven. Be perfect in your heart, weed your garden, and take that envy out of your heart. It was for envy that they crucified the Lord of Glory. They are going to crucify you. But you've got to understand covetousness. If Pilate knew, then you've got to know. You've got to know the score – they are covetous out there.

So how do we rise above it? First, understand it through self-examination. Why do you have depression? Why do you behave the way you behave? Why are you oppressed? You should keep a clean garden and be transparent. Repent of covetousness when you find it. When you allow yourself to be cleansed by the washing of the water and the Word of God and allow yourself to be examined in light of the Word of God, you've got nothing to hide and you can walk above their criticisms when they say things about you. I'm not saying that words don't hurt us. But the key here is self-examination in light of the Word of God.

The Ten Commandments are deep. Some people want to walk away and say, "We are under grace, not under law; therefore, we do not need to follow the Ten Commandments." Do you know the damage you inflict on yourself by allowing yourself to break these commandments? Paul said, "God forbid that I allow sin." They accused Him of the very thing that people accuse me of, that because we are under grace, the law doesn't matter. Go ahead and sin.

No! Paul said that's not what I'm preaching. I am preaching grace, but grace is also the fulfillment of the commandments. Because we could never keep them, Jesus had to die on the cross. He had to suffer such an agonizing payment for our sin so that we could be made the righteousness of God in Christ Jesus. If righteousness were of the law, He didn't need to die, but He had to die because these things seep into us. They take root in us. But when we want to press on towards perfection and be like Jesus, we will spend the time and allow the Word of God to be written upon our heart by the spirit of grace instead of upon tablets of stone. We obey by faith.

But are you allowing the spirit of God to write the Word of God on your heart? Examine yourself. You must answer to God on this question. Are you allowing God to write His word on your heart? Are you allowing the spirit of God to come into your soul and become part of you? Or are you just being religious? Because if you are, you are just walking in a shadow. You are observing ceremonies, not following the Spirit of God. If this is you, the best thing you can do is to pray. It will take time. Real Christianity takes time to grow in you. God has come in and rescued you. He will save and bless you. Pray that God will grow in others and take that covetousness away from them.

Let's look at the story of Joseph and his brothers. What was the problem with his brothers? Let's look at the Bible:

And the patriarchs, being envious, sold Joseph into Egypt, but God was with them. (Acts 7:10)

It was out of envy that his brothers sold Joseph into slavery, but God was with him. So if people come against you, if you are blessed of God, then you can know also that God is with you.

How should we respond in this age that we are living in? We are living in rough times. This is the time for us to know Jesus, to have God with us, to experience the blessings and favor of God. At times, others will be envious of us because of the Spirit of God that rests upon us, because of the beauty and perfection of God's holiness that is revealed within us. But you've got to keep your passion for the things of God, even if others persecute you as they did Jesus and Joseph.

Don't stay in the doldrums. Don't look at other Christians and covet what they have. Don't think that you will be happy if you have what they have. No, you won't. You are not meant to have what they have, but are meant to have what you have. The scripture says, "Thou shalt not covet your neighbor's house. Thou shalt not covet your neighbor's wife, nor his male servants, or his female servants." Don't envy even if they have a gardener, a maid, and own a corporation. Those things don't matter. Don't covet his ox, or his donkey, or anything your neighbor has. I have a beautiful dog, Connie. Don't covet my dog, okay? Get your own dog.

On the other hand, there are good things to covet. The bible says in I Corinthians, "covet the better gifts," and to "covet to prophesy." You should want to speak under the anointing of God. If you want to covet something, these are the things to want, to covet after. Covet after spiritual things, not the carnal things. If you will seek first the kingdom of God and his righteousness, everything will be added unto you and you will have an abundant and full life. Look at this next scripture:

> But fornication and all uncleanness or covetousness,
> let it not even be named among you as is fitting for
> the saints. (Ephesians 5:3)

Be careful about this, he says. Don't be wanting the things of someone else in the church. He is writing to the Christians. And then he says:

> ...neither filthiness, nor foolish talking, nor course
> jesting, which are not fitting, but rather the giving of
> thanks. For this you know that no fornicator, unclean
> person, nor covetousness man, who is an idolater, has
> any inheritance in the kingdom of God.
> (Ephesians 5:4-5)

To be covetous means you are an idolater. You have set up an idol. 1 John says stay away from idols. Being covetous is idolatry. It is an idolatrous action that takes place in your heart, and that changes you from having your eyes on God to having your eyes on man and his things.

You might never go after those things, or purposely steal them; but if it's in your heart, then you already have. Jesus talks of adultery like this, that even if you lust with your eyes, you have committed adultery already. We know in James, that lust and envy are the beginning of sin. In Jesus' eyes, when we go deeper with this command and go into the spirit of covetousness, you are not on the path of life. You are certainly not in peace, because the presence of God brings the peace of God Lastly, you are not strong. The anxious person is the weak person.

When you get into a place of covetousness and you believe that everyone has it better than you, you need the Word of God to come into you and prune your heart. Jesus says you are clean by the washing of the water of the Word. We have got to get into the Word of God and pray daily and be disciplined. Not out of religion, but to follow the spiritual things, to nip covetousness in the bud. Even Paul was covetous, although you might not think he was:

> What shall we say then, is the law sin? Certainly not? On the contrary, I would have not known sin except through the law. For I would have not known covetousness unless the law had said, "Thou shalt not covet." (Romans 7:7)

Paul was coveting those early Christians. Remember Jesus was crucified out of envy; Joseph was sold into slavery out of envy; and Paul had Stephen and those other early Christians killed out of envy. Paul studied the Word of God and was a Pharisee of Pharisees, and yet he was not experiencing the power of God. Paul wanted what they had; and if he couldn't have it, he would kill them. But God had mercy on him. And God will have mercy on us if we repent and seek His face. He can turn someone else from being a covetous Saul into being another mighty apostle Paul.

Conclusion

What is God saying to us when we look at the Ten Commandments and try to put them all together? I really think it's a lifestyle of worship. It's a lifestyle of being in love with Jesus. A lifestyle that says, "I want to please the Lord. If something offends Him, it offends me."

In this final chapter, we will now tie all the commandments back together to see the whole picture. Just as when I was in my nursing program and it wasn't until the sixth term that I understood the importance of the earlier terms and how they each related to the later terms. We will now recap and summarize each of the commandments, while connecting them into a single, cohesive set of laws which only when brought together (into God's perfect "Top 10" list) can we fully know and understand God's good and perfect will toward us and for our lives. We begin with Commandment #1, which states the first truth of the Law, as well as the first truth of our very lives: that God, and God alone, is our Lord, Creator, Giver of Life, and Savior.

Commandment #1:
I am the Lord your God.
You shall have no other gods before me.

In Commandment #1, from Exodus chapters 19 and 20, we learned that the big thought in this Commandment was when God spoke these words, "I am the Lord your God, who brought you up out of the land of Egypt, the house of bondage, and you shall have no other gods before me." The real emphasis here is what a wonderful privilege it is to be part of the people of God. We don't want to have any other gods before Him.

Now, what happens when you go around and start worshipping something that isn't God? You've got a "sin" thing going on in your life. You don't have a problem, you've got a sin thing. You're missing it; you're off track; things are breaking down in your life; you don't have it together. Where is your first love? He said you will have no other gods before me. People don't want to hear that part, that you can get lukewarm or cold. Now if you can get lukewarm, that means you can get cold. So we want to emphasize here what a privilege it is that we know he is the Lord our God, and we will have no other Gods before him."

We are special people. We are in a privileged position. This is a wonderful commandment. This is awesome; I love God and I'm His. I love the prayer, "I'm yours, and yours I wish to be." This is great. Desire nothing else, my friend. God likes this. This pleases Him. Do you want to know what pleases Him? When you love Him with all your heart and soul, when he's your God. Let God be your God. Let God arise, and let His enemies be scattered.

One time a woman called me up, and said, "I'm really being tempted to fly and meet my boyfriend in Los Angeles. They weren't married. "What should I do?" Hello, that is a no brainer. I said, "Let's both pray about it for a week, and we'll talk about it again in a week." I wanted her to come to this decision on her own, thinking that God is more important than this creature. I called her in a week, and said, "You called me last week and wanted to know whether you should fly to Los Angeles and meet this guy. I asked, 'What do you think?'" I was so let down. She said, "I've chosen to live life dangerously." I said, "What?" I said "That is wrong; you're not married." She chose to live life dangerously.

When you don't want God to be God, you are living dangerously, and you get out from under the shadow of His wings. There is protection under the wings of the Lord. But when you say I don't want God to be God in my life, those wings just flap right in. You are not under the shadow of his wing, and that is dangerous. Let's start life on the right foot by knowing, understanding, believing, and living in this truth that God is our Lord, and no other gods in our lives will come before Him.

Commandment #2:
You shall not make for yourselves graven images...
You shall not bow down to them or serve them.

The second commandment deals with his presence. It says, "You shall not make for yourselves graven images...shall not bow down to them or serve them...for I am a jealous God, visiting the iniquity...but showing mercy to thousands who love me and keep my commands." Now, what is he really saying here? Is it really about the piece of wood, or the golden idol? No, it's relationship. It's putting that thing before God. Maybe it's some possession that you have. God is jealous; he's your lover. That's the thing He is talking about there.

In the Song of Solomon, there is the verse, "I'm my beloved, and He is mine...His banner over me is love." But if you are going after this other thing, He's a jealous God. If my wife Peggy started dating another guy, I'd probably be nuts. I'd get real jealous. "What are you doing, you're married to me!" "Oh, but I like him, he's cute." "Hey, I am too!" (Or I try to be). It almost makes you feel for God, because He's jealous. Let's go back to God. Let's look at the positive side. That means He loves you! Don't make any idols to worship; worship God alone.

Commandment #3:
You shall not take the name of the
Lord your God in vain.

Let's look at Commandment #3. Do everything in His name. I love it. "You shall not take the name of the Lord your God in vain, for the Lord will not hold him guiltless, who takes his name in vain." Is it about cursing? I don't think so; that's way too superficial. You know what it's about? To me, this is scary because this really hit me. It's when we pray in the name of Jesus, but it's really in vain. It's when we take the name of the Lord in vain – not in faith. We shouldn't be praying in the name of Jesus and using the name of Jesus and everything that it represents, the authority, the command, the reputation of God, but then not believe in the name and not be representing the name in honor.

When Peggy took my name in marriage, she chose to represent me where she would go. We represent God whereever we go. Like in a marriage, we take the name of Jesus and we're not going to go and ruin His reputation in the community. Don't marry Him and go and trash the name of the Lord and go commit adultery out there, spiritual adultery. No, He doesn't like that. It's good to know He doesn't like that.

We are holy people. That means don't be taking that name in vain. Don't be taking it like it's worthless. It's precious. At the name of Jesus, every knee will bow one day and we're going to see it happen. We choose on this side to bow to the name. But I can't stand it when I'm in a theatre, and they use that name in vain in a movie. What do I do? I will praise the name of Jesus and say, "Oh Jesus Christ, He is Lord, Hallelujah, I will praise Him." And I love it. See, if they're going to take the name in vain, I'm going to praise it. I don't care who is sitting next to me or behind me. Let them hear me – maybe that's the only time they'll hear praise to God. In everything you do in the name of the Lord, do it with honor, give God the glory, and do not let his name be taken in vain.

Commandment #4:
Remember the Sabbath Day, to keep it holy.

Commandment #4: "Remember the Sabbath Day, to keep it holy. Six days you shall do ....for in six days the Lord made the heavens and the earth. And he rested..."

102

Remember what the conclusion was there? What's the real meaning? Is it really about not doing any work on Saturday? I don't think so. The real key here, for those who have eyes to see and a spiritual understanding, is that God rested on the seventh day. The work of Christ is finished. It isn't about works; it's about the finished work. We are to rest in hope. We are to labor to enter into the rest.

Now you might say, "Pastor Frank, that's an oxymoron, you're working to enter into the rest." Well, you want to know something? If you don't dig into the Word of God, I don't care how wonderful you are, you are not going to grow. And you cannot live on yesterday's bread. You've got to eat daily bread: "Give us this day, our daily bread." I've got to be in that Word every day. I've got to labor to enter into that rest. I have to get up in the morning and seek God with all my heart and pray. You can ask my family, who know that I am disciplined. I do that No glory to me because my flesh doesn't always want to do it, but I just know I'm going to do it. I've been trained. And once I get in there, I like it, though. It's like, "Oh, I'm glad I do this; this is the way to begin my day." And you know what? When I labor to enter into that rest, the day is good. He seems to take care of it for me. If there is a problem, he's gone ahead of it for me.

You see, I'm trusting God. That's what it means to enter the rest of God. You're trusting the Lord. He doesn't like when you trust the arm of the flesh. That's what this commandment is about. Who are you putting your trust in? Are you putting your trust in you, or are you putting your trust in the arm of the Lord? I say let's trust in the Lord. Let's cease from our labors, and go ahead and take the time to enter into the rest.

Commandment #5:
Honor your father and mother.

Let's look at Commandment #5. "Honor your father and your mother, that your days may be long upon the land, which the Lord your God is giving you." This is deep. I remember when I said to my congregation, "You know I'm not excited to preach this, because this seems like a boring scripture." But by the end of the message, guess who got it? I began to see more clearly. You see, it really is about honoring life. God honors life. Parents represent life-bearers They represent God to us. When you disrespect them, it's like you disrespect God. And if you as a father or a mother don't expect respect from your child, you're missing it. They need boundaries.

Children need to know that you are the authority figure in that home. If you let them get away from it, because "Oh, that poor baby," that's wrong. God doesn't like that, because God chastises those whom He loves. He says if you spare the rod, you will spoil the child. Am I talking about abuse? Absolutely not! I'm talking about a God who takes the time to correct me. I thank Him that He does, and I must correct my children.

God's a loving God, but I want to tell you, He has taken me to the shed a few times. When I really did wrong, "Oooh," I said, "Daddy God," and He said, "I'm "Father." Right now, you sit up and you listen to me. That was wrong what you did." I liked that, and I came out of the shed and said go ahead any time. I want to be right with you, and I want to be corrected when I'm wrong. I don't want to live wrong or with some illusion.

He says it will go well with you in life. You are going to live long if you live this. This is like a temporal promise. And guess what? This country has fallen apart because the home has lost its strength. The devil got into the family life. I wish I could paint a prettier picture for you. But in the United States of America because the homes are weak, the country is weak. The country was stronger when the country had strong homes with mom and dad still together. But when parents are on their third or fourth marriage, with three kids from three different marriages, plus one from someone that they weren't even married to, some are afraid to discipline their kids because, God forbid, the children might be offended. Well maybe the children need a little offense. Maybe those parents need to wake up and smell the coffee and say, "Hey, this isn't right, you've got to be pleasing to God." Now, I'm not saying Jesus doesn't love these families, just as Jesus loved the woman who was divorced five times and was with someone new who wasn't her husband. But what I'm saying is that we as a Christian body and church need to make families strong. We need to encourage families. We need to encourage the disciplining of the children. We need to love the children, and we need to receive their respect. It's all okay. It's good with God.

I encourage us to stand up for righteousness' sake in this hour. It still is not too late. Respect the life-givers in your own life, and teach your children to respect you as parents, and your family will have long life and happiness.

Commandment #6:
You shall not murder.

Commandment #6: Thou shalt not murder. This is a basic one. Hate in your heart is equal to murder. Jesus equated that. You may never kill someone physically with a gun or knife, but you can kill them with your words. Sticks and stones can break my bones, but words will never hurt me. Forget it; that's a lie. Words hurt. Words wound. Sometimes people remember words more than physical pain. When you bruise the soul, it's harder to heal than the body when its bruised. Watch those words. But you say, "I've got to speak. It just comes out of me. I'm just that type of person." Well, then change. You can change because that's not pleasing to God. We want to please God. We want to understand the depth of the concept, rather than simply the superficiality of the commandment. Loving other people and treating them with tender mercies and grace, rather than with hatred or ignoring them, is the way to avoid being a murderer.

Commandment #7:
You shall not commit adultery.

Commandment #7: Do not commit adultery. Now that's kind of obvious. But let's go deeper, remember? Weren't we talking about spiritual adultery, about unfaithfulness to God? Wasn't it about if you are married to Christ and you go off and you are unfaithful, and you come back to Christ, and you are unfaithful again, and you come back to Christ again, and you repeat it over and over again. Yes, he is merciful, but I want to tell you something. That is just like a whore, a harlot who goes out and commits adultery with a man. But you are doing it in a spiritual sense. It's talking about growing up. When you are tempted to go out and have your little petty sin pleasure because you've just got to have it. You supposedly can't help it, because it's a stronghold. Come on. A lot of those strongholds aren't strongholds. All you've got to do is to say no. Admit it and quit it. You've still got a free will.

You do not have to engage in sin. That breaks off your relationship with God. That's spiritual adultery and God does not want that. And we can mature and grow up and be strong. When you become spiritually mature and that thing comes along and tempts you away from God to filthy yourself, something in yourself says, "Not this time, not this time, because I see it. I'm married to Christ. I'm my beloved's, and He is mine. And His banner over me is love." God forbid that I drag that banner into some whorehouse and commit spiritual adultery in some sin factory. Let's take some responsibility. Can I write to you like strong believers?

Commandment #8:
You shall not steal.

Commandment #8: Do not steal. What was the message there? What does it say in Ephesians: "You who stole, steal no more. Work with your hands that you may have something to give." What's the opposite of stealing? Giving it? Working hard with your finances and giving something away, because you labored with your hands instead of just stealing from someone.

It's an abomination to take what's someone else's, because it represents a part of their life. With God, it's a part of their life because they had to work. They had to labor. We are a little more used to labor for two weeks, and then you get a check, but it was for your labor for those two weeks. Years ago, they had to work on the farm and get that produce and sell it to get their needs. If someone took something they owned, it was really evident that they took of another person's sweat and blood, which they had given to earn their money to buy that thing. When you take that thing, you are taking a part of their life. We don't have the right to do that.

We cannot enter in and take what is somebody else's. On the other hand, we have the right to use our life's blood, our energy to work hard and to bring the first fruits into the kingdom, to have tithes and then offerings, and to grow the kingdom. What a privilege to say "God, I've labored for you all week, and I get to give this money into the offering." I find that to be great joy. Or, if someone has a special need and you hear about it, and you sweated for them, you labored for them...you gave them a part of your life.

Commandment #9:
You shall not lie or bear false witness.

Commandment #9: No lying or bearing false witness. Why? Because of the truth. Jesus says I am the truth. We bear the truth in our heart. How can we tell a lie when we are supposed to be an ambassador of truth? How can you enter into a situation and lie, speak a falsehood, and then claim to be of the truth? God doesn't like that.

Commandment #10:
You shall not covet.

Commandment #10: Thou shalt not covet. What is the meaning behind this? I pointed out that some didn't think it was as bad, because it wasn't really the completion of an act. When you steal, you really take something from another. But when you covet, it's really a heart thing. I want it, and I don't want them to have it. I want what they have.

But you see, that is even worse, I believe, than actually taking what they have. Jesus was crucified because of the covetousness of the Sadducees and Pharisees. You see, they didn't want him to have that spiritual authority. They wanted to be the high priests. They wanted to be the one in authority. And guess what? God doesn't like that. He wants us to rejoice when someone else is blessed. He wants us to be happy when they are promoted, to rejoice with those who rejoice, and to sorrow with those who sorrow. He doesn't want us coveting what they have, and say, "I've got all the spiritual gifts. They just haven't discovered me yet." Instead of saying, "Wow, that person is anointed, they speak to my heart."

Some Final Thoughts...

In conclusion, as you now understand, it is so very important to know God's commandments. It is important to know the law of them, and to know, understand, and be able to effectively apply the spirit and principles behind them, rather than leaving them buried in the Old Testament, never to be read.

Perhaps you feel condemned when you read them because maybe you steal a little or still lie a little. Maybe you are into that spiritual adultery thing. Maybe you have hate in your heart. Maybe there is something you really love and you can't let go, and you love it more than you love God. Maybe you are hating your mother and blaming her for everything that went wrong in your life. Don't ignore these

108

areas or convictions you feel where you know you are breaking the commandments. I say if there is something wrong there, go ahead and let it bubble up. It will even be a little painful. But that's how healing comes. It comes up, the soulish healing, the inner healing. Then repent of the thing, because God made a way, when there was no way, to forgive and to heal and to bring reconciliation and wholeness.

Now, that you have read this book and are armed not only with the laws of God's "Top 10 List" but also God's spiritual principles behind them, go out into your daily life and start experiencing the freedom and the joy of the Lord, joy unspeakable and full of glory. I'll go so far as to say you can have heaven on earth: "Thy kingdom come on earth, as it is in heaven." Where you are, that's where the kingdom is. He says, "The kingdom is within you." He will help you live by the kingdom's principles many of which are so beautifully revealed within God's Ten Commandments of the Bible.

About the Author

Rev. Frank Julian RN BSN graduated from Grand Valley State University in Grand Rapids, Michigan, in 1977. He has worked primarily with the physically disabled and in geriatric home care during the last 28 years.

Frank married Peggy Eskro ,who is also a nurse, in 1978 and they have 2 children. Their daughter Angela Harris, married to Dustin, is a graduate from the University of Michigan, Ann Arbor, and is a chemical engineer with Ford Motor Company. Their son, Frankie, is in Pharmacy school at the University of Michigan.

Frank is a pastor at Faith Christian Assembly and was ordained by the Christian Church of North America in 1997.

Frank is an Aids Activist and when asked to send liquid nutrition to the suffers of the disease on a trip to Botswana in 2001, he responded. He has formed a non-profit organization called, FAWN: Fighting Aids with Nutrition. As of 2005, 14 shipments weighing 60,000 lbs. have been sent to South Africa (7) and to Botswana (7).

Frank's claim to fame is his $10,000 smile. He won $10,000 in the McDonald's smile marathon in August 2000, smiling for 7 hours and 43 minutes.

This is the first book Frank has authored.

How to Order

God's Top 10 List,
Rev. Frank S. Julian, RN, BSN

Website orders:

www.buybooksontheweb.com

Toll-Free Telephone orders
(Canada and U.S. only)

Call Infinity Publishing's bookstore
(Buybooksontheweb.com)
1-877-289-2665